The Kirwan murder case, 1852

Maynooth Studies in Local History

SERIES EDITOR Raymond Gillespie

This volume is one of five short books published in the Maynooth Studies in Local History series in 2019. Like their predecessors they range widely over the local experience in the Irish past. Chronologically they focus on the late eighteenth and nineteenth centuries but they focus on problems that reappeared in almost every period of Irish history. They span the experience of rebellion in late eighteenth-century Dublin and the trauma of family relations and murder in the early nineteenth century. More mundane tasks such as the problem of managing the poor, the task of economic development through the shaping of infrastructure and the management of land also feature. Geographically they range across the length of the country from Dublin to Waterford by way of Carlow and westwards from Howth to Sligo. Socially they move from those living on the margins of society in Sligo through the urban middle classes of mid nineteenth-century Dublin to the prosperous world of the urban elite in Waterford. In doing so they reveal diverse and complicated societies that created the local past and present the range of possibilities open to anyone interested in studying that past. Those possibilities involve the dissection of the local experience in the complex and contested social worlds of which it is part as people strove to preserve and enhance their positions within their local societies. It also reveals the forces that made for cohesion in local communities and those that drove people apart, whether through large scale rebellion or through acts of inter-personal violence. Such studies of local worlds over such long periods are vital for the future since they not only stretch the historical imagination but provide a longer perspective on the development of society in Ireland and help us to understand more fully the complex evolution of the Irish experience. These works do not simply chronicle events relating to an area within administrative or geographically determined boundaries, but open the possibility of understanding how and why particular regions had their own personality in the past. Such an exercise is clearly one of the most exciting challenges for the future and demonstrates the vitality of the study of local history in Ireland.

Maynooth Studies in Local History: Number 141

The Kirwan murder case, 1852
A glimpse of the Irish Protestant middle class in the mid-nineteenth century

Suzanne Leeson

FOUR COURTS PRESS

Set in 10pt on 12pt Bembo by
Carrigboy Typesetting Services for
FOUR COURTS PRESS LTD
7 Malpas Street, Dublin 8, Ireland
www.fourcourtspress.ie
and in North America for
FOUR COURTS PRESS
c/o IPG, 814 N Franklin St, Chicago, IL 60610

ISBN 978–1–84682–801–0

Printed in Ireland
by SprintPrint, Dublin.

Contents

Acknowledgments

I wish to thank the many people whose work, research and guidance made this book possible. In particular, I express my sincere gratitude to Harriet Wheelock, Keeper of Collections in the Royal College of Physicians of Ireland Heritage Centre for her help in accessing their collection of William Burke Kirwan's anatomical illustrations and her advice on literature relating to Dublin's golden age of medicine. I would also like to thank the staff of the National Library of Ireland particularly Mary Broderick, Assistant Keeper of Special Collections, for her valuable assistance while viewing the Kirwan collection of painting and sketches. In addition, I extend my appreciation to the staff of Fingal Public Libraries, particularly those in the Howth branch for their provision of materials relating to the history of Howth. Finally, I wish to acknowledge my family, whose help and support during the writing of this book was invaluable.

Introduction

On 10 December 1852, William Burke Kirwan, a Dublin artist,[1] was convicted of the murder of his wife Sara Maria Louisa Kirwan three months earlier on Ireland's Eye, an island off the fishing village of Howth, Co. Dublin, and sentenced to death.[2] Kirwan's conviction followed a trial of just two days, was based entirely on circumstantial evidence, heavily dependent on medical testimony and witness statements and, with hindsight, containing many inaccuracies and inconsistencies. Despite no direct evidence produced to convict him, contemporary newspapers seemed convinced of his guilt, as did the prosecution and the public. His extra marital relationship with Teresa Kenny, with whom he fathered seven children, and which continued throughout his marriage to Sarah,[3] provided a motive for her murder, was heavily capitalized on by the prosecution and, in the press and in part, contributed to the guilty verdict.

This case and Kirwan's conviction was immensely controversial. Committees were founded to mount a public campaign to petition for his release, letters of protest appeared in the British press[4] and pamphlets in Kirwan's defence and in support of the guilty verdict were circulated in Dublin.[5] Following a storm of public condemnation of the verdict, Kirwan's death sentence was commuted to transportation for life, and he spent 27 years in prison, in Ireland, London and Bermuda, until his release in 1879.[6] The controversial nature of the evidence, the doubts about the guilty verdict and the scandal caused by Kirwan's domestic arrangements have ensured that this case has held an enduring appeal. Several writers of the time attempted to defend Kirwan while others supported the verdict, and newspapers at home and abroad took differing views on the case and conviction. In the over a century-and-a-half since the murder, case and trial, it has continued to have a hold on the public imagination. The persistent mystery surrounding the murder have led several authors to attempt to 'solve' it, while others discuss its role in criminal history or its contentious nature.[7] Today, the story of Sarah Kirwan's death has evolved into somewhat of a folk tale,[8] a notorious murder mentioned to add colour to the frequent summer boat tours to Ireland's Eye.

While the evidence in this case will be briefly reviewed in this book and readers may draw their own conclusions as to Kirwan's guilt or innocence, it is not the purpose of this study to finally reveal the truth of Sarah Kirwan's death. For the historian, an examination of the Kirwan case and the subsequent public reaction gives a glimpse of the wider Dublin middle-class society of the

1. Howth village with Ireland's Eye in the background, 1860. James Simonton and Frederick Holland Mares, 'Thatched cottages in foreground, sea, Ireland's Eye in background, Howth, Co. Dublin' (the Stereo Pairs Photograph Collection, NLI, STP_0857)

mid-19th century. However, despite a brief mention in a survey of Howth's local history spanning several centuries,[9] this author was unable to locate any specific academic historical analysis of the case. To that end, the Kirwan case and the social commentary it provoked will be examined, and this research will show that it provides a representation of the strata of society to which he belonged, namely the Dublin Protestant middle class of the mid-19th century, and embodies many of the attitudes and values that they subscribed to.

Kirwan's links to Dublin's senior medical establishment through his work as a medical illustrator will be explored and the achievements of those known as the Dublin school of medicine will be discussed. The importance of medical evidence in this case will show the growth in influence of the emerging field of medical jurisprudence in criminal trials throughout the 19th century. This case's influence on a campaign for a full British Court of Criminal Appeal will also be considered. Following commutation of his death sentence, Kirwan was transported to Bermuda and life for prisoners in the penal colony will be explored alongside Kirwan's treatment there, and his handling by the Irish administration when the system of penal transportation was ended in 1857.

Sarah Kirwan was a Catholic, her husband a Protestant and while this was not laboured upon in court or indeed appears not to have encroached on their marital life, their differing religions was a theme used in defence literature and by the newspapers, who emphasized this distinction. Her role as a middle-class woman will be explored in relation to her childlessness at a time when societal discourses around motherhood portrayed it as the highest aspiration for women of all classes. The legal rights of women of the mid-19th century will be considered through Sarah Kirwan's experience as a woman who may have experienced domestic violence, married to an unfaithful husband and through the treatment by society of Theresa Kenny, her husband's mistress, after their liaison was revealed. In addition, the public reaction to the exposure of Kirwan's double life as an unfaithful husband and father of illegitimate children will be discussed. Newspaper reporting played a large role in portraying Kirwan as immoral and the salacious press coverage of his conviction for murder and his lifestyle provides a contemporary view of prevailing moral codes and of crime reportage, which had increased in popularity up to the mid-19th century. This fascination with crime, particularly murder, will also be discussed in relation to the case.

1. The Kirwan murder, case and trial

'Being moved and seduced by the instigation of the devil'[1]

On the morning of 6 September 1852 William Burke Kirwan and his wife Sarah were brought by boat to Ireland's Eye, a small uninhabited island off the fishing village of Howth, Co. Dublin, where they had been holidaying since the middle of June.[2] Kirwan, an artist, and Sarah had been married for 12 years and were an affluent couple living in fashionable 11 Merrion Street Upper in Dublin, home to many of the city's legal and medical professionals.[3] Howth, in 1852, was a small fishing village approximately seven miles from Dublin city with 692 inhabitants, concentrated mainly in just one main street.[4] A new harbour, built by the Scottish engineer John Rennie, was completed in 1817, and served as the main location for the mail packet ship route to Holyhead until 1834, when its unsuitability for large vessels meant the route was transferred to Kingstown.[5] Despite this, the Drogheda and Dundalk Railway Company opened a branch line to Howth from Dublin in 1846, with a terminus station situated directly on the harbour by June 1847.[6] This rail line would be particularly beneficial to Kirwan as he commuted daily to the city throughout his stay in Howth.[7] The railway company took out advertising in the newspapers encouraging 'cheap pleasure trips' from the city to Howth, extolled the virtues of its 'wild dells, romantic bays and magnificent headlands', the 'beauty and sublimity of scenery' and promoted sea bathing by offering reduced rates of one penny for the use of bathing machines on purchase of all rail tickets.[8] Given average wages paid to skilled workers in Dublin were 20s. per week, ticket prices beginning at a shilling for a day return[9] put these pleasure trips out of reach for most of the working classes, making this mainly a pastime for the middle classes and above. Notwithstanding this, the trips proved so popular that by July 1847 the railway company were required to introduce extra Sunday trains due to the increased passenger numbers coming from the city, and the *Freeman's Journal* reported in mid-July that on the previous Sunday, almost 1,000 passengers were conveyed by train to Howth, with a further 1,000 making the trip by steamer.[10] By 1852, a large hotel occupied the waterfront.[11] Picturesque Ireland's Eye, less than a mile off Howth harbour, was a particular attraction, described in an 1842 travel guide as 'the famous little island', with its sixth century ruins of the chapel of St Nessan, early 19th-century Martello tower, rare sea birds and views of the coast.[12] Popular for day-trips, the Kirwans had been to the island several times during their holiday in order that Kirwan could paint and Sarah sea-bathe.[13]

2. Unfinished watercolour of Ireland's Eye by William Burke Kirwan (NLI, 2085TX(148))

Sarah was said to have been particularly fond of sea-bathing since her childhood, having been advised to practice it for her good health, and was reported to be a strong and adventurous swimmer.[14]

The Kirwans remained on the island throughout the day, and were observed by several witnesses.[15] The Brew family, who spoke with Sarah a number of times during the day, had offered to take her back to Howth when they were leaving at four o'clock but she declined, stating that she and her husband were being collected four hours later.[16] The Brews duly left and the Kirwans were alone on the island until local boatmen Thomas Giles, Edward Cavanagh and brothers Patrick and Michael Nangle came to collect the couple at 8 o'clock that evening. Kirwan was alone sketching at the landing place on their arrival, and when he informed the boatmen his wife had gone to bathe earlier and he hadn't seen her in some time, they suggested that the island be searched. Patrick and Michael Nangle accompanied Kirwan, and after two searches Sarah's body was found, lying on a rock in an area of the island known as the Long Hole.[17] After the body had been transported back to the mainland at Howth, in the absence of a local doctor, it was examined by James Hamilton, a medical student, who concluded that Sarah had died by drowning as he did not observe any marks of violence on the body. A coroner's inquest was subsequently held the following day, 7 September, returning a verdict of accidental drowning.[18] Sarah Kirwan was buried in Glasnevin Cemetery four days later.[19]

From the beginning suspicion fell on Kirwan for the murder of his wife and several people came forward expressing disquiet over the coroner's verdict of accidental drowning, while Kirwan's behaviour after Sarah's body was found was deemed suspicious.[20] A neighbour of the Kirwans and self-professed personal friend of Sarah, Maria Byrne, on reading a report of the inquest in the newspaper, came forward with the suspicion that Kirwan had murdered his wife, having made attempts on her life in the past.[21] The Nangles related that when they arrived on the island to collect the couple, Kirwan was found at the landing place, calmly sketching, although by that time it was very dark and when questioned as to the whereabouts of his wife, he answered that he had not seen her for an hour-and-a-half.[22] Kirwan's boots, trousers, stockings and underwear were observed by them to be wet and they noted that this did not happen when returning by boat to Howth.[23] Kirwan insisted that Sarah's body be washed on its return from the island to their lodgings in Margaret Campbell's house and despite being admonished by Ann Lacy, a local nurse tender who viewed the body there and advised him that the police may not want it touched until an inquest could be adjourned, Kirwan stated 'I do not care a damn for the police or anybody else; the body must be washed'.[24] In addition, a fisherman, Thomas Larkin, informed the Wicklow police that he heard screams coming from the island as he passed on the day of the murder and when the inquest was reported in the newspapers, they reported this to their Dublin counterparts.[25] Larkin's evidence was corroborated by four Howth residents who also heard the screams, each from different areas near the harbour.[26] Reports also surfaced that Kirwan had, during his marriage, been leading a double life, dividing his time between his wife and a woman named Theresa Kenny, who lived in Sandymount with their seven children and it was suggested that this other family had been moved into his Merrion Street house after Sarah's death.[27] This led the police to reopen the case and Sarah Kirwan's body was exhumed and a post mortem performed, resulting in evidence that suggested that she had been strangled.[28] Kirwan was then arrested on suspicion of her murder and a private government enquiry, chaired by the inspector general of the Dublin constabulary, Major Brownrigg, was held in Howth to examine witnesses.[29] Following this enquiry, on 26 October, Kirwan was charged with Sarah's murder, to which he pleaded not guilty.[30] The case opened on 7 December 1852 and from the beginning was a cause célèbre, with large numbers of the public queuing from an early hour to be admitted.[31] One newspaper remarked that 'great anxiety was manifested by those present to obtain a view' of the accused and another proclaimed that the excitement caused by the trial in Dublin was 'without any parallel in the present century'.[32] After two days of evidence from 22 witnesses for the prosecution and 2 for the defence, following one night of deliberations, the jury returned a guilty verdict and Kirwan was sentenced to hang, his date of execution fixed for 18 January.[33] Kirwan, who throughout the trial was reported as calm and composed, vehemently protested his innocence on passing of the death sentence, stating that 'I never had hand act nor part in, or knowledge of my wife's death'.[34]

That Kirwan's conviction for murder scandalized Dublin society was unsurprising; premeditated murder was rare in mid-19th-century Ireland, with rates well under those of England and Wales.[35] Murder rates had decreased since the 1840s, with women making up less than 10 per cent of all those killed between 1842 and 1860.[36] Kirwan was one of just 14 individuals convicted for murder in 1852, and the only one in Dublin.[37] The case was controversial, attracted huge public interest, and was extensively reported in the press in Ireland, the United Kingdom, New York and even as far away as Australia.[38] The salacious nature of Kirwan's infidelity added a frisson of excitement, attracting large public interest, stirred up by newspaper reports exuding moral outrage about his 'hardly disguised and habitual adultery' and capitalized on by the prosecution, which played up his connection of an 'illicit and immoral character with another woman'.[39] The prosecution, led, by coincidence, by a Merrion Street neighbour of Kirwan's, George Smyly, contended that Kirwan had strangled his wife before abandoning her to be swept out to sea.[40] The defence, led by Isaac Butt, acclaimed barrister and future founder of the Home Rule Association, asserted that Sarah had drowned as a result of swimming too quickly after eating, exacerbated by her apparent epilepsy, which she inherited from her father.[41] However, this author can find no evidence to support this statement. On the contrary, Sarah's father James Crowe's death in 1844 was found by an inquest to be caused by heart disease and his wife, Maria Crowe, in a statement to the crown, never mentioned that either he or her daughter suffered from epilepsy.[42]

As the conviction was based on circumstantial evidence, some newspaper editorials condemned the verdict as 'a hasty judgment dignified by public opinion' and letters of protest began to appear in the British press.[43] Two separate pamphlets in Kirwan's defence were circulated in Dublin, authored by a Reverend Malet, Trinity College scholar and close friend of Kirwan and by John Knight Boswell, a solicitor, who took a personal interest in the case and attempted to argue against the evidence and discredit much of the rumour published by the newspapers.[44] A further pamphlet which attempted to justify the guilty verdict by analysing the medical evidence produced at the trial was published by Thomas Geoghegan, a professor in the Royal College of Surgeons who specialized in medical jurisprudence.[45] Pamphlets such as these played an important intellectual role in Dublin society in the first half of the 19th century as an effective vehicle to stimulate public debate and for the conveyance of political, religious and economic issues before being superseded from 1850 by the growth in newspaper journalism.[46] Public meetings were held in Dublin and London for those opposed to the verdict and committees were formed in both cities to protest against the sentence.[47] The London committee resolved to send a deputation to wait upon the secretary of state for the home department to register a personal protest against the verdict, writing to request a meeting, which was subsequently refused.[48] Letters from across Ireland and Great Britain were also sent to the lord lieutenant petitioning for clemency.[49] Isaac Butt, Kirwan's defence lawyer, requested in parliament that a bill be brought in to grant a full court of criminal appeal hearing that could order new trials in cases such as this, where the evidence was ambiguous and one newspaper suggested that 'something must be done for the improvements of Irish inquests and juries on criminal cases'.[50] Such was the storm of protest that jury members published letters reaffirming their belief in Kirwan's guilt, stating that the circumstantial evidence against him was overwhelming and it was this and not Kirwan's long-term infidelity that caused them to convict.[51] In contrast, the coroner's inquest jury foreman added to the debate, emphasizing their verdict of accidental death, expressing his belief in Kirwan's innocence and noting the inconsistency of his detention, when the remission of the capital sentence had, in effect, acknowledged he did not commit the crime.[52]

Kirwan was granted a reprieve by the lord lieutenant, Lord Eglington, on 1 January 1853 and his sentence was commuted to penal transportation for life,[53] which prompted further public debate. Some Irish newspapers condemned this as a mistake and suggested that the lord lieutenant had pandered to British public opinion while others called for the foundation of a court of criminal appeal to avoid such an outcome in future.[54] Such was the outcry and public demand as to who engineered the commutation of sentence that the under secretary to the lord lieutenant addressed a note to be printed in the newspapers clarifying that it was the judges of the case who recommended this course.[55] Although the lord lieutenant personally reviewed petitions for mercy on behalf of a convicted felon, a recommendation of mercy by the judge who presided over the case could considerably improve their chance of commutation of sentence.[56] Lord Eglington's decision to commute Kirwan's death sentence would not have been unusual as the percentage of executions carried out for murder convictions had been decreasing in Ireland as the 19th century progressed, with just 48 per cent resulting in death between 1846 and 1850.[57] However, Eglington would later admit to having reservations about the commutation of sentence, and based on these doubts, in 1858, while in his second tenure as lord lieutenant, would refuse a petition by Kirwan for remission of his sentence.[58]

Controversy continued during Kirwan's subsequent imprisonment, with questions raised regarding his treatment. Kirwan was held in Kilmainham Prison, Dublin where he was reported to have a spacious apartment, separate from the prison population, access to a large exercise yard, his choice of food and was not required to wear prison clothing.[59] In addition, it was reported that prison staff delayed two constables who were investigating Kirwan's possible past crimes and who wished to search his cell, allowing him to burn incriminating documents.[60] This favoured treatment he received in Kilmainham would result in the resignation of its deputy governor, following a government enquiry into Kirwan's handling by the prison authorities.[61] Kirwan was transferred from Kilmainham Prison to Spike Island, Cork harbour, a convict transportation depot,[62] on 10 January 1853, and remained there for several months. However, even the manner of his transportation to Spike Island was a matter of public debate and it was noted with condemnation that he travelled in

3. Spike Island showing the prison, a traditional six-bastioned military fort, built *c.*1790 (Cork County Council)

a private carriage, was not handcuffed and wore a cloak and hat over his prison uniform, leading the *Freeman's Journal* to comment that 'there is one law for the rich and another for the poor'.[63] Spike Island was a relatively new prison, opened in 1847 and was originally intended as a temporary detention centre for a few hundred prisoners en route to Britain's penal colonies.[64] However, by 1852, when Kirwan arrived on the island, it had grown substantially, and with 2,300 prisoners, was severely overcrowded.[65] Housed in what was originally a military barracks, lack of space required that prisoners slept together in large wards, partitioned each side by wooden boards and wired to the front.[66] McCarthy and Ó Donnabháin suggest that, by the 1850s, in terms of prisoner numbers, Spike Island, unprecedented in scale and size, had become the largest convict establishment in the world and one of the first 'super-prisons'.[67] As a member of the middle class, Kirwan was in the minority, as between March 1849 and September 1850, 85 per cent of inmates received by the prison were from the labouring classes.[68] Newspapers once again questioned Kirwan's presumed preferential treatment in the prison, where he was reported to be staying in a 'comfortable apartment', had permission to paint, and was permitted 'all the comforts and luxuries he can procure with money'.[69] One newspaper observed that this lack of punishment was 'very strange and inexplicable', and called for an enquiry to investigate, remarking that they hoped it was not because a distinction was being made because of 'rank, creed or class'.[70] These reports necessitated another government statement, with the prison's office in Dublin Castle publishing a letter from the governor of Spike Island in the newspapers denying this, stating that 'Kirwan is treated in every respect as a normal felon'.[71] Further accounts detailed this treatment, that he shared a dormitory with up to 30 people, dined on prison food and was engaged in hard labour pumping water for the prison.[72] The assurance that Kirwan's handling by the prison authorities conformed to regulations was repeated six months later when it was reported that he was 'employed on Spike Island at the most severe truck labour and is not allowed any special indulgence of any kind'.[73] Kirwan was transported to Bermuda on 13 April 1854, aboard the convict ship the *Amazon,* where, despite several petitions for remission of his sentence and reports from prison staff of his exemplary conduct, he remained until the breakup of the convict settlement in 1863, following the cessation of the penal transportation system.[74] Kirwan left Bermuda aboard the *Gerard Seymour* on 25 March 1863, returning to Spike Island via Millbank Penitentiary in London to serve the remainder of his sentence.[75] He was finally released on 18 January 1879, leaving a prison with a much reduced population of just over 514 convicts by the end of that year, and one which was on the verge of closure. Spike Island would eventually close in 1883, reverting to its original purpose as a military post.[76]

2. The Kirwans' life in Dublin

'I am an artist, residing at No. 11 Upper Merrion Street, Dublin'[1]

William Burke Kirwan was 36 years old at the time of the murder and in 1852 he had been married to Sarah for 12 years.[2] Son of a Fermanagh picture dealer, Patrick Kirwan, and described as a miniature painter, his family home was at 2 Parnell Place in Harold's Cross.[3] Kirwan enjoyed a varied career before his conviction, originally training as a medical student, before studying art under the tutelage of the portrait and miniature painter, Richard Downes Bowyer.[4] He experienced some modest success, exhibiting in the Royal Hibernian Academy of Art (RHA) from 1836 to 1846.[5] In a review of their annual exhibition of 1842, Kirwan was described as a 'meritorious native artist' of 'vast talent' whose painting 'must have cost the artist considerable time and labour in its perfection'.[6] Incidentally, a fellow exhibitor on that occasion was Thomas Bridgford, who would go on to become a member of the RHA and a reputable portrait painter in Ireland and the United Kingdom.[7] His father, also Thomas, together with another son ran a successful nursery business in Spafield, Sandymount, and was also the owner of several houses there.[8] One of these houses was rented by Kirwan for Theresa Kenny and their children and Thomas' son William would later give evidence in court to that effect.[9]

A collection of Kirwan's paintings and sketches held by the National Library of Ireland contains several of his watercolours from this time, some of which show scenes of rural Connemara and one of which, 'The dairy maid' (fig. 4), was described after it was exhibited in the RHA as 'a clever picture' which was 'attractive and well painted'.[10] Kirwan's links to the RHA may have enabled him to gain employment with the Ordnance Survey Office, colouring maps from the first ever survey of the entire island of Ireland, which was carried out between 1829 and 1846.[11] George Petrie, noted landscape artist and antiquary, who was a member of the RHA Council since 1830, was appointed to the topographical department of the Ordnance Survey in 1833.[12] By 1836, although still residing in Parnell Place, Kirwan had taken rooms in Dublin's South King Street with the purpose of working for the Dublin district of the Ordnance Survey, who completed their survey of the city in 1837 with the first of the Dublin maps published in 1840.[13] A sketch in the National Library collection appears to be made on a printed cover sheet of one of these early maps, given that it states that the surveyor was Lieutenant Bordes, who was responsible for overseeing the Dublin city survey, beginning in 1836.[14] In addition to this work, combining his

4. 'The dairy maid' by
William Burke Kirwan,
1843, watercolour (NLI)

medical knowledge and artistic skill, Kirwan also found work as an anatomical
draughtsman in Dublin's hospitals, while also maintaining a lucrative sideline as
a portrait and landscape painter.[15]

An incident before Kirwan's marriage may give an insight into his character
and foreshadow his unfaithful behaviour during his marriage. In 1839, he was
accused of seducing a respectable young woman and was challenged by her
brother to marry her or fight a duel.[16] A rare practice in 1839, duelling would
largely die out by the middle of the 19th century and although legal, it was
frowned upon by Dublin's middle-class Protestant society, considered to be an
antiquated tradition and an immoral and un-Christian social evil comparable
to drunkenness and gambling.[17] The woman's family also posted placards and
letters around Dublin, giving Kirwan's name and address, details of his conduct,
'unprecedented in the annals of crime' and warning other families against him.[18]
In an echo of the language of the plethora of newspaper reports that would
condemn Kirwan thirteen years later, he was denounced as a 'thoroughbred
poltroon' and the woman described as 'the victim of his demoniacal passion'.[19]
Kirwan, although not denying an acquaintance with the woman, denied
seducing her and took a case for libel against her brother, although it appears
that this was more an attempt to protect his reputation as the case did not go to

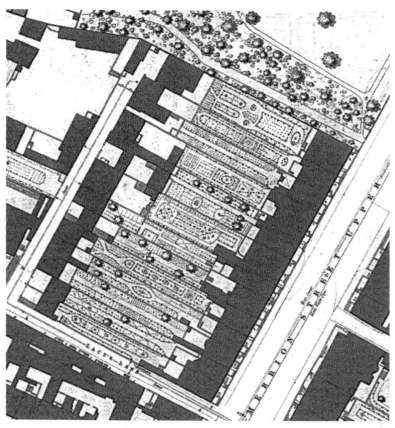

Map 1. Merrion Street Upper in 1847[22] (© OSI)

trial. He would marry Sarah Crowe in October of the following year.[20] Kirwan had also been before the courts two years before, accused by Anne Bowyer, wife of Kirwan's mentor Richard Downes Bowyer, of assaulting her in her home, stealing money and a savings book and kidnapping her husband.[21] Although this case also did not proceed to a trial as the judge instructed the parties to reconcile the matter between themselves, this and the previous case would resurface after Kirwan's conviction in 1852, cited as an example of his previous immoral life and of the supposed heinous crimes that he had committed in his past.

The Kirwans appear to have had a relatively affluent life. After their marriage, they lived in 13 D'Olier Street until 1844 and then in the Dublin townhouse of Kirwan's father at 6 Merrion Street Lower, before moving to their own home at 11 Merrion Street Upper around 1851.[23] Adjacent to the wealthy and fashionable enclave of Merrion Square, home to nobility, gentry and the Dublin professional elite, the Kirwans' immediate neighbours mainly consisted of legal professionals.[24] They appeared to be prospering, the house in Merrion Street

Upper, described in one newspaper as 'a fine mansion', was certainly larger than their previous home, possessing an office, yard and small garden and with a leasehold value of £110 per year was over twice the £50 leasehold value of their old home.[25] Also, reports of a public auction of the Kirwans' possessions after his conviction note that they included a gold watch and chain, 'a six octave square piano', several coats and jackets, a quantity of muslin dresses and bonnets, a book collection and a large amount of artwork.[26] In addition to the house on Merrion Street Upper, Kirwan owned three properties on Clare Street, leased from the Pembroke estate which gained him an income of £205 per year, and lands in Ryne, Co. Longford which produced £150 annually.[27] After Kirwan's conviction these houses and lands were sold by public auction for £4,505, and all monies were forfeit to the Crown Treasury.[28] Despite his income from property, Kirwan's main occupation was as an anatomical draughtsman and portrait painter.[29] After his trial it was reported that he earned £1,000 a year as an artist, when the average weekly wage in 1851 for agricultural labourers in Leinster was 5s. and the annual wage for skilled labourers in 1867 was approximately £52.[30]

Kirwan also kept a mistress, Theresa Kenny, their seven children and a servant in a rented house in Sandymount and at the time of Sarah's murder they had been in this relationship for 12 years.[31] Although his politics are unknown, he may have had moderate nationalist tendencies, evidenced by his signature in 1848 on the petition for clemency for the Young Ireland leader William Smith O'Brien, who had been sentenced to death for treason.[32]

Less is known about Sarah Kirwan. Described in newspaper reports after her death as 'an extremely respectable lady' and 'remarkably handsome', she was from a Catholic family and the eldest child of James and Maria Crowe, retired lieutenant of the 2nd West India regiment.[34] Born in Peter Street, Dublin, in March 1820, from 1830 the family resided at 30 Beresford Street,[35] in the north of the city. Sarah's father had led a somewhat unusual life up to Sarah's marriage. Originally enlisted as a soldier in the Clare militia, he was commissioned as an ensign, the lowest infantry rank, in the 2nd West India regiment in 1813 and promoted to lieutenant in 1816, seeing service in America and Jamaica before retiring on half pay due to ill health in 1817 and being posted to the 2nd garrison battalion in Dublin.[36] It was far from uncommon for an Irishman to volunteer for the British army, in 1796 there was 50,000 serving Irish and between 1793 and 1815 up to 159,000 Irishmen joined English regiments.[37] However, at that time Catholics were usually restricted to the ranks of the militia at home in Ireland or after the lifting of an official ban in 1799, enlisted in the army as regular soldiers. James Crowe, as a Catholic, would have been in the minority in the 19th-century British army officer class, which was dominated by sons of the Anglo-Irish gentry and in which Catholic officers regularly made up less than 5 per cent between 1827 and 1865.[38] Furthermore, his commission was without purchase, or on merit, when the majority of commissions were purchased, making a career as an army officer unattainable for many ordinary Catholics

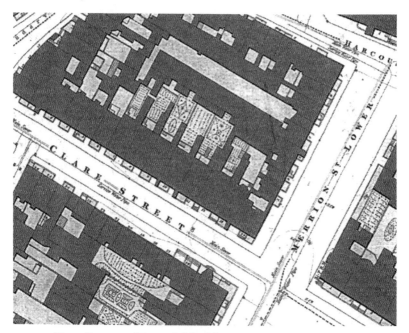

Map 2. Location of Kirwan's father's house at 6 Merrion Street Lower
and his rental homes on Clare Street[33] (© OSI)

and restricting it to the sons of wealthy Irish Protestants or the few Catholic
elite who wished to reinforce their loyalty to the crown and gain a means of
social advancement.[39] Notwithstanding his religion, that Crowe did not buy his
commission was certainly unusual when, between 1700 and 1871, most Army
commissions were bought.[40]

Crowe's family background may, to some extent, account for this. He
claimed to be son and heir to Robert Crowe, a wealthy Protestant landowner,
holder of large estates in Co. Clare, which in 1819 produced an income of
£3,000 per annum.[41] His alleged father, apparently married his mother, Sarah
O'Brien, while an inmate of the Dublin Four Courts Marshalsea debtors
prison in 1787 and they lived together in Dublin on his release in 1788. James
was born in 1790 and when his mother died in 1793 his father remarried soon
after, whereupon James was given into the care of a family in Wicklow and
apprenticed as a shoemaker. Crowe was unaware of his parentage until after
his retirement from the army and on learning that, although his father had
remarried, he had no children, James instituted a series of court cases to prove
his legitimacy and right to inherit as Robert Crowe's sole male heir. Crowe's
first case was heard in Ennis in 1819, and had the distinction of having Daniel
O'Connell, future Catholic nationalist leader and champion of the Catholic
Emancipation and Repeal campaign, then at the height of his legal career, as

part of his legal team.[42] Despite this, the court found against him, which led
Crowe to petition the chief secretary's office in 1821 complaining that he had
been defrauded of his inheritance, pleading poverty and requesting financial
aid or government employment which would enable him take a further case.[43]
Referring to his excellent military conduct and recommendation by the duke
of York (then the British army's commander-in-chief), he pleaded for help to
'alleviate my wretched condition' by granting him a situation or 'asylum in
the Royal Hospital of Kilmainham'.[44] Although it is unknown whether Crowe
received any help, financial or otherwise, he pursued his case twice more, first
in 1822, when he once again retained O'Connell,[45] and then again in 1823.
As he was unsuccessful on both these occasions, he appears to have accepted
the verdict of the courts. However, in the following years the Crowe family
seem to have been living in straitened circumstances, given the contents of a
remarkable pamphlet published by Crowe in 1835,[46] five years before the
Kirwans married. Part begging letter and part public plea for employment, it
contains correspondence with the Catholic bishop of Kildare and archbishop
of Dublin, who had attempted to petition Lady Wellesley, wife of the duke of
Wellington and herself a Catholic, for assistance on his behalf. Although this was
unsuccessful, she provided £2 to Crowe to assist in the education of his children
and the bishop of Kildare and archbishop of Dublin pledged an annual donation
of £5 and £2 respectively. The pamphlet also contains Crowe's correspondence
with the earl of Shrewsbury, another prominent Catholic peer, whom he had
waited on in London requesting help to find a place in the Royal Military school
for his son, but again to no avail.

Testimonials in the pamphlet from prominent Protestant ministers R.J.
McGhee and Gideon Ousely stated their belief in Crowe as a respectable
gentleman and as the lawful heir of the estate in Clare.[47] However, despite
Crowe's avowed rank and respectability from his connections to Clare landed
gentry and previous service as an officer in the British army, the family appear
to have lived in genteel poverty. According to his pamphlet, Crowe had not had
employment since his retirement from the army in 1817 and remained attached
to the 2nd garrison battalion in Dublin on officer's half pay.[48] British army
officers were not entitled to a pension until 1871 and half pay was, in practice,
a fee paid to retain the officer as long as he held a commission, while, in theory,
they remained available for future service.[49] As Crowe was not commissioned
by purchase, he did not have the option that many officers took on retirement
of selling their commission, making up for their lack of a pension. Raising
five children without employment to supplement this half pay must have been
financially difficult as army pay rates were low; for example, a captain's full
rate of annual pay was £283 in 1832.[50] Crowe admitted in his pamphlet that it
was 'ill-suited to supply present necessities' and he was unable to provide his
children with 'an education proportionate to their rank'.[51] The family's rented
home on Beresford Street was situated in one of the most overcrowded areas of

the city, St Michan's Parish, an area that had some of the worst slum dwellings in Dublin and in 1841, had an average of 16.5 persons per house, with half of the families who lived there occupying just one room each, exceeding overcrowding levels in the London slums.[52] Predominantly working class, it was described by Thomas Willis in his survey of the area in 1841 as 'the refuge of reduced persons from other districts', and he noted that 'there are no gentry within the district, and the few professional men or mercantile traders whom interest may still compel to keep their offices here, have their residences in some more favoured localities'.[53] Willis revealed the unsanitary conditions in the tenement buildings of the various lanes and courts of the district, which he declared were 'unfit for the residence of human beings', in a state of filth and disrepair and therefore rife with disease.[54] Although the Crowes lived in a house and their neighbours were predominantly skilled tradespersons, as can be seen on the Ordnance Survey map of 1847 (Map 3), the Crowe family home, number 30, was in close proximity to four of these aforementioned courts as well as being adjacent to Stirrup Lane, which Luddy notes was the site of one of Dublin's many brothels.[55]

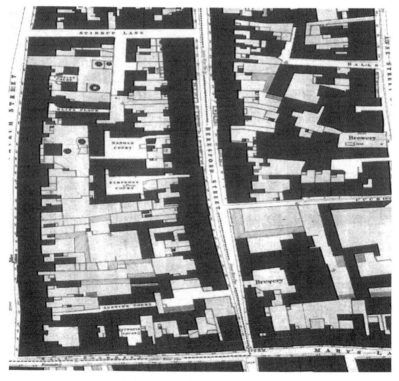

Map 3. Beresford Street 1847; the Crowe home is at number 30 at the intersection with Stirrup Lane[56] (© OSI)

Given the evidence of the Crowe family's precarious financial situation, there can be little doubt that marriage to William Burke Kirwan, a Protestant gentleman with a regular income, lodgings in town and family residences in Harold's Cross and Merrion Street Lower, was considered an advantageous match. Moving to the newly built and wide thoroughfare of D'Olier Street and then on to the heart of the professional city, the spacious Merrion Square area, with its wide carriageways and flagged paving, would certainly be considered an improvement from what David Dickson terms 'the city of rags'.[57] Sarah married Kirwan on 20 October 1840, by special licence, in the Church of Ireland parish of Rathfarnham.[58] The procuring of a special licence from the bishop, although expensive, avoided the calling of banns for the previous three weeks before the ceremony, giving the advantage of a quicker wedding and affording the couple privacy[59] and while this may have applied in this case, that it was a mixed marriage may also have played a part. That the marriage was performed by a Protestant clergyman ensured that the marriage was legal as mixed marriages performed by a Catholic priest were by law considered void.[60] This arrangement would have been acceptable to the Catholic Crowe family as a marriage not performed by a Catholic priest between a Protestant and a Catholic had been recognized as valid by the pope since 1785.[61] Sarah reportedly remained in constant contact with her family throughout her marriage,[62] perhaps unsurprising given their pecuniary situation.

However, mixed marriages were rare in early 19th-century Ireland and counselled against by leaders of both churches.[63] Despite this, they were accepted as legally valid and a custom, known as the 'Palatine Pact', existed that the male children followed the father's faith and the females, their mothers.[64] Attitudes against mixed marriages would harden considerably from mid-century onwards and the Catholic Church under Paul Cullen, archbishop of Dublin from 1852, was particularly hostile to such unions.[65] Despite this, Sarah Kirwan did not convert to Protestantism and according to her mother, freely practiced her religion, without interference from her husband.[66] Theresa Kenny, Kirwan's mistress was also reported to be Catholic and according to her brother Nicholas, in contrast to Sarah Kirwan, she had converted to Protestantism during their relationship, causing a rift among her siblings.[67]

There are conflicting reports regarding Sarah's knowledge of the existence of Kenny and her children. The prosecution suggested that she discovered her husband's infidelity not long before the murder, thus causing disharmony in the marriage and giving Kirwan a motive for murder, while in contrast Kenny stated that Sarah knew of her existence for 10 years.[68] This was confirmed by Caroline Bentley, a friend of Sarah's, who stated that Sarah was aware of Kenny less than a month after her marriage and she regarded 'his intimacy with Kenny as the only fault in his character', and by witness testimony of Sarah's acquaintances during the Kirwan's Howth stay.[69] Notwithstanding this, the Kirwans' marriage was reported by others to be harmonious. Bentley reports that Sarah repeatedly

5. Sketch by William
Burke Kirwan,
notation on the rear
'Mrs Kirwan sketched
by her husband'[73]
(NLI)

told her that 'a more quiet gentle, good natured or generous man never existed', insisting that she frequently mentioned his kindness and tenderness towards her.[70] Kirwan's assistant of 14 years, a Mr Kelly, in a statement to the crown states that he was not aware of any negative comment from Sarah regarding her husband, insisting that he never heard 'thro any channel that Mrs Kirwan complained of the conduct of Mr Kirwan's towards her, on the contrary'.[71] Her mother concurred, stating that Kirwan could not have been 'a more sober, quiet and industrious husband' who supplied her daughter with her 'every want and desire' and treated her kindly, while they lived a life of comfort and respectability suited to Sarah's 'rank and station in society'.[72]

Maria Crowe stressed that Kirwan consented to and publicly supported her daughter's wish to attend Catholic services.[74] This was a somewhat atypical attitude at that time when, in 1848, regarding Ireland, the diarist Charles Greville noted that, 'Protestant bigotry and anti-Catholic rancour continue to flourish with undiminished intensity'.[75] Furthermore, many Protestants at that time held deep-rooted suspicions regarding the growing influence of the Catholic Church.[76] Dublin's Protestants numbered 30 per cent of the city's inhabitants by the mid-19th century and while there was a working class, which made up 44 per cent of all Protestant males in Dublin, the majority were of the middle class and above.[77] Kirwan as a member of the middle class would have been among the social hierarchy of the city, enjoying much of its power, wealth and influence.[78] However, after Catholic emancipation in 1829, the social and commercial status of the Dublin Catholic middle classes began to rise, culminating in their gaining control of Dublin Corporation from the early 1840s and resulting in increased polarization of the religions in the city as the privilege of the minority began to be gradually eroded.[79] Although the Kirwans' religious denominations were not alluded to in the trial, in contrast to the religious tolerance reportedly within the Kirwans' marriage, the sectarian undercurrents present in society began to appear after the murder conviction.

Boswell, in his defence pamphlet, refers to Howth's Catholic parish priest, Fr Hall, who on the return of Sarah Kirwan's body from the island, pointed to Kirwan and told the police sergeant to 'keep your eye on that man'.[80] Although loath to include this evidence for fear of bringing a 'religious tone to the case, so much to be dreaded in this country', he nonetheless reminded readers that 'the whole of the evidence on which Kirwan was convicted was that of the humblest class in society', reminding them that in the 'social condition of this country', to this class the priest's word was law.[81] This, he implied, meant that whether Kirwan was guilty or not, once the priest voiced his suspicions, his parishioners, the boatmen and other witnesses from Howth, were sure to follow his example. This idea that Catholics were in what Hill calls 'bondage to their priests and the pope' and tutored by them to be anti Protestant was a familiar theme throughout the 19th century, expressed often in Protestant society, alongside appeals for the evangelization of Catholics.[82]

Religious prejudice was also present in newspaper reports. An editorial in *The Nation*, an influential nationalist newspaper and organ of the Young Ireland movement, referred to those who sought Kirwan's innocence as 'the Souper interest'.[83] Souper was a derogatory name for a proselytizing Protestant, whose giving of charity was dependent upon the Catholic recipient's conversion, a practice that caused particular resentment among Catholics during and after the Famine.[84] The article suggested as a motive for murder that Kirwan was a 'man of violent Orange principles' and that his wife had converted to Catholicism some months prior to her death, a 'fact' disproved by her mother's statement.[85] This led to a letter of protest in the *Dublin Evening Mail*, a Protestant newspaper, denouncing this article as slander and asserting that this attitude was key to Kirwan's conviction, as the case had become, 'as every question of more than a few weeks' duration is sure to become in Ireland', 'an ecclesiastical quarrel'.[86]

The *Waterford Mail*, another Protestant newspaper, added to the debate by suggesting that it was Kirwan who had converted from Catholicism to Protestantism and as his wife was Catholic, the jury, which they proposed consisted of 11 Catholics and one Protestant, was biased against him and convicted him because of 'the vindictive feeling that exists against a man that abandons one religion for another'.[87] No evidence can be found for this statement, although the Kirwan's marriage was announced in the *Dublin Morning Register,* a pro-Catholic emancipation newspaper.[88] Although it is unknown if Kirwan himself was a convert, many Catholics did convert in the 18th and early 19th century to avoid the effects of penal legislation, facilitate better opportunity or improve their social status.[89] However, the theory regarding Kirwan's conversion was condemned as a 'gross insult' and the report was dismissed as 'eminently mischievous' by the nationalist *Cork Southern Reporter*, and described as a 'grievous and mortifying blunder', whose only aim was to excite sympathy for Kirwan in 'the Protestant mind', written by 'an obscure scribbler or two in an obscure rag', by the nationalist *Dublin Evening Post*.[90] Reports of this nature led to yet another newspaper statement by a member of the administration, this time the crown solicitor, William Kemmis, who stated that the jury was a mixed panel of 'partly Protestants and partly Roman Catholics' and defended their 'intelligence and impartiality'.[91] This was followed by a letter from one of the jury, who also refuted the claims by the *Waterford Mail*, stating that at least five of the jury were, to his knowledge, Protestant.[92]

Kirwan's work as an anatomical draughtsman and medical illustrator brought him into close contact with several of the city's noted surgeons and physicians. By the time of his conviction medicine was one of Dublin's elite professions, with many of its distinguished members living close to the Kirwans in Merrion Square. The departure of the aristocracy from the city after the Act of Union in 1801 left a social vacuum, which was filled by the professional classes, not least physicians and surgeons.[93] By the mid-19th century the medical profession had evolved from apothecaries and barber surgeons, regarded as trade, into a prestigious career for respectable professional gentlemen, who considered themselves part of society's upper echelons.[94] Despite the social rise of the Catholic middle classes since the beginning of the century, the medical world was still overwhelmingly Protestant and entry to this elite world was limited for Catholics.[95] Even with the establishment of the Catholic University Medical School at Cecelia Street in Dublin in 1854, the medical profession, especially at the top level, was dominated by Protestants and census figures from 1861 show they comprised 70 per cent of surgeons and 66 per cent of physicians. Places in the leading Dublin hospitals were limited and the majority of Catholic graduates worked as local doctors in the dispensary service or for the armed forces and the imperial service.[96]

The prestige of the profession was, in part, due to the many medical advances made in Dublin in the early 19th century and Kirwan lived through and worked in what is considered 'the golden age of Irish medicine' with advances in surgery and practice that influenced Europe and America.[97] At the end of the 18th century, Dublin had one of the highest number of hospital beds per person in the United Kingdom and further new hospitals continued to be built throughout the 19th century, providing opportunities for teaching and innovation.[98] The achievements of the 'Dublin school of medicine' created an international reputation and by 1861 the city was at the forefront of medical education in Britain, attracting over 1,000 medical students from Europe, America and India.[99] Irish doctors founded the Irish Medical Association in 1839, in an effort to advance the profession through clinical research and discussion, while the *Dublin Medical Press*, established the same year, promoted its professionalism, respectability and authority.[100]

Chief among the many prominent Dublin physicians and surgeons of the time, comparable to today's top consultants, were Sir Dominic Corrigan, William Stokes, Robert Graves and Francis Rynd. Corrigan, one of the few Catholics in the profession, was physician to Queen Victoria in Ireland and made discoveries in cardiology, including heart murmurs and irregular pulse during disease, still known today as 'Corrigan's Disease' and 'Corrigan's Pulse', respectively.[101] Stokes specialized in thoracic disease and pioneered the use of the stethoscope to detect chest conditions, while introducing a new, more collaborative style of clinical teaching.[102] Graves revolutionized the treatment of fevers by stressing the importance of a nourishing diet.[103] The catch-all label of 'fever', consisting of a large group of diseases, largely unknown in the early 19th century, was the biggest killer of Irish society, accounting for one in five of all deaths.[104] Along with his work with fever patients, Graves is best known today for his diagnosis of what is still known as 'Grave's Disease', a thyroid gland condition.[105] The invention of the hypodermic syringe in 1845, to facilitate direct delivery of medicine into the body, is attributed to Rynd.[106] Other notable luminaries of the Dublin School included Sir William Wilde, father of the playwright Oscar, a pioneering eye surgeon, who founded St Mark's ophthalmic hospital in 1844 and developed techniques and instruments relating to aural medicine, Sir Henry Marsh, founder of the first Dublin hospital for children's disease and Robert Adams, later Surgeon to Queen Victoria, who became known as 'the revered father of Irish surgery' and specialized in arthritis of the joints.[107] Kirwan's surviving medical illustrations, some of which are held in the Royal College of Physicians of Ireland, primarily relate to skin diseases and are the result of his employment by William Wallace, dermatologist, specialist in venereal disease and founder of the first hospital in the United Kingdom and Europe exclusively for the treatment of ailments of the skin.[108] Wallace was recognized by his contemporaries for his innovative research on the treatment of syphilis with iodine and the discovery of the contagiousness of secondary syphilis.[109] A painting by Kirwan, held in the National Library's collection, illustrates this work, showing the development of syphilitic pustules.[110]

Given Kirwan's work, religion and place in society, it is not inconceivable that the Kirwans, being neighbours (Graves, Corrigan, Stokes and Wilde all resided in Merrion Square),[111] were part of some social gatherings in Merrion Square and mixed with these elite members of society. Dublin Victorian doctors showed an appreciation for the artist in society and patronized the arts.[112] William Stokes entertained an eclectic range of guests alongside the doctors and

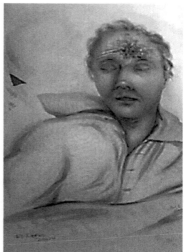

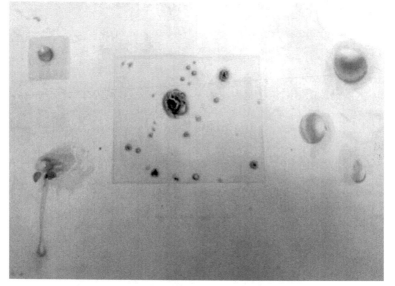

6. Examples of William Burke Kirwan's medical illustrations of skin diseases, clockwise left to right, Kitty Stapleton, 1848 and Thomas Eames, 1841 (Royal College of Physicians of Ireland Archive); syphilitic pustules (NLI)

lawyers of his acquaintance and his home was regularly frequented by writers, actors and particularly artists.[113] Kirwan's association with these higher echelons of Dublin society would have added to his own prestige and position. However, this connection would also have added to the 'shock-value' of his arrest, trial and conviction. Despite this, after Kirwan's conviction, many senior members of the medical profession came forward in his defence, disagreeing with the medical evidence presented at the trial. Robert Adams and Francis Rynd gave testimony in court for the defence, the only witnesses called, and Rynd also added his name to pamphlets circulated in Dublin aiming to clear Kirwan's name.[114] Graves and Marsh also gave their names to this document alongside other senior medical professionals of the city.[115]

Kirwan's trial was heavily dependent on 'expert' medical evidence, a feature of mid-19th-century criminal trials.[116] The growing field of forensic medicine was in its infancy but would gain authority throughout the 19th century, and have a large influence on legal and judicial decisions.[117] This was also the era when the idea of what Tony Farmar terms 'doctor as sage'[118] or the holder of a deep insight began. Medical practitioners held a unique place in criminal trials in the 19th century, given this insight, their service to society and their assumed professional authority, and it was common practice in criminal trials that their scientific evidence was invoked as fact with little attempt made to prove otherwise.[119] In this case the opposing sides each produced medical experts. The prosecution's medical witness was Dr George Hatchell, physician, police surgeon, and surgeon to the lord lieutenant's household,[120] while the defence produced the aforementioned Rynd and Adams. It is indicative of the esteem afforded to medical evidence in criminal trials that theirs was the only defence testimony given in court.

After the verdict, a proliferation of 'eminent' experts was produced on both sides, who declared their opinion on the medical evidence. Medical professionals feature in the many petitions for clemency to the lord lieutenant, including one from the Medical Society of Liverpool.[121] A pamphlet endorsing the medical evidence, in support of the guilty verdict, was published by Thomas Geoghegan, professor of forensic medicine, and fellow of the Royal College of Surgeons, purporting to be a full exposition of the medical 'facts'.[122] In contrast, Malet included the testimony of ten Dublin physicians and surgeons in his pamphlet, who asserted their belief in Kirwan's innocence based on the medical evidence.[123] Boswell also included 'expert' evidence from Albert Swaine Taylor, a doctor, toxicologist and a leading expert in medical jurisprudence, who consulted on the case on the recommendation of John Moore Neligan, physician to Jervis Street Hospital and future president of the Royal College of Physicians of Ireland.[124] The aforementioned opinions show that Kirwan had the support of a significant section of the Dublin medical profession, particularly those in the higher ranks of the profession and of society. Both Malet and Boswell present these doctors' sworn testimony as statements of absolute fact, to legitimize their argument for Kirwan's innocence. Again this was common practice in criminal trials in the 19th century where statements made on oath as to what was heard and seen were accepted at face value as the truth and little attempt was made to prove otherwise.[125] This can be seen in the trial, where testimony given by Howth locals, that screams were heard from the island at the supposed time of Sarah Kirwan's death, was not verified or refuted by either the prosecution or defence.[126] Doubt was only cast on this evidence after the trial when two gentlemen, reported as academic professionals, performed an experiment on the island, one discharging several pistol shots at the Long Hole, none of which was heard by his companion, who waited at the landing place.[127] The amount of medical opinion, albeit of differing conclusions, and the dependence on it by those for or against Kirwan's conviction, emphasizes the eminent role the physician held in society, what Watson refers to as men of 'professional authority',[128] men of education and social standing whose elite position ensured their opinion was valued. This is confirmed by the writer John Gamble, in his account of visiting Dublin in the early nineteenth century, who, commenting on the social status of physicians, state that they 'are almost at the pinnacle of greatness' and alongside the legal profession, 'form the aristocracy of the city'.[129]

3. Sarah Kirwan and the role of middle-class women in society

'A female – a helpless unprotected female, one whom by the laws of God and man was entitled to your protection'[1]

Despite this 'golden age of Irish medicine', and the many advances achieved by the Dublin school, from her mother's statement[2], it appears that Sarah Kirwan was taking several herbal remedies that may have been severely toxic. Mrs Crowe recounted that her daughter was taking large quantities of tincture of henbane, prescribed to her by an apothecary.[3] According to the Kirwans' landlady in Howth, Margaret Campbell, she was also in the habit of taking comfrey root and sage.[4] Henbane, a powerful narcotic, gained fame in the early 20th century when it was used by Doctor Crippen to poison his wife.[5] Henbane is a psychoactive substance, so poisonous that the smell of the flowers can produce dizziness and overdose can cause vomiting, delirium, hallucinations and seizures.[6] It was, however, a common medicine in the 19th century, included in an Irish pharmacopoeia, favoured by Queen Victoria and described by Pierce, in a domestic medical book, as beneficial in 'allying pain' and 'arresting spasm'.[7] Similarly, comfrey root, also a popular remedy, boiled in water to make a tea, can also be toxic, causing liver and kidney damage, while concerns have been raised about the poisonous effects of long-term use of sage.[8] Use of each one of these herbal remedies could have contributed to Sarah Kirwan's demise. However, it is the reason that these medicines were normally prescribed at the time that is of note, as each medicine in some way was prescribed for menstrual problems. Henbane was prescribed for painful and heavy menstruation, sage for irregularity and calming of the uterus while comfrey was recommended for all menstrual problems, particularly what was known as 'female debility', or menstrual discomfort.[9] Additionally, sea-bathing, which Sarah had been recommended to take up 'as necessary for the preservation of her good health, was medically prescribed at the time as an aid to increasing fertility.[10]

The pervading societal discourse throughout the 19th century was that the highest aspiration for women of all classes was marriage, where she would be subordinate to, and dependent on, her husband and her main function in the union would be a reproductive one.[11] This attitude is clearly shown in Malet's defence of Kirwan where he implies that, because Sarah was childless, she would regard Kirwan as 'almost suffering wrong or injury'[12] because of her lack of fertility, and would be more disposed to turn a blind eye to his infidelity.

The suggestion was that Sarah had disappointed her husband by her failure to fulfil the role of motherhood, seen as a vocation[13] or a sacred duty with women's innate feminine characteristics particularly suited to the task. Mothers were idealized as selfless, caring, nurturing women, who helped maintain the social order by instructing their children in the moral and religious values and proprieties expected of their class.[14] Given this ideology regarding motherhood, after 12 childless years it is possible that these remedies and swimming regime were undertaken by Sarah Kirwan in an attempt to conceive, particularly if she was aware of the existence of her husband's seven children with his mistress.

The discovery of the existence of Theresa Kenny was inferred by the prosecution as the provocation for an episode of marital violence witnessed by Margaret Campbell, the Kirwan's landlady in Howth. Previously observed to argue more than once, on that occasion, Kirwan was overheard calling his wife a strumpet and saying 'I'll finish you' while she asked him to 'let me alone, let me alone'. This evidence was corroborated in court by Anne Hannah, a visiting neighbour, who revealed that she heard Kirwan say the words 'I'll end you, I'll end you'. The following morning Sarah was overheard telling her husband 'she was black from the usage she had got the preceding night'.[15] Unremarked upon at the time, the incident was only recounted by Campbell after Sarah's death, and it was dismissed by Malet as a quarrel.[16]

Although Campbell stated in court that despite having witnessed at least four arguments, Kirwan had 'never used violence but the once',[17] witness statements found in the trial documents seem to imply otherwise, relating that, according to Sarah herself, rather than being a solitary incident, caused by the revelation of her husband's double life, domestic violence was an ongoing feature of the marriage. Maria Byrne, a neighbour of the Kirwans from Lower Merrion Street, gave a sworn statement to the crown on 23 September. In her evidence, she detailed her suspicions that Kirwan had murdered his wife and alleged that on two occasions he had attempted to poison her, first with alum, a pickling spice, and then with henbane. She stated that on the first occasion, six years before, Sarah herself had told her she 'lived a very unnatural life with her husband' and because he was frequently absent from the home at night she suspected he had another family. On the second occasion, Byrne maintained that Kirwan instructed Sarah to take tincture of henbane, resulting in her being in 'a dangerous state' for six weeks, contrary to Sarah's mother's claim that this medicine was prescribed for her daughter by one of her relations, an apothecary.[18] During this time, Byrne claimed, Sarah was near death and attended by a priest from Westland Row chapel, while being treated by the aforementioned physician Francis Rynd, a situation which led her mother, Maria Crowe, to threaten to have Kirwan prosecuted if her daughter died and to speak to both a priest and a constable about the matter.[19] Even though this statement was given in sworn testimony to the crown, when Rynd gave medical evidence in court, he was not questioned about this incident, stating only that he attended Sarah for a fever six years before, and Crowe denounced Byrne's evidence as 'wholly false and unfounded'.[20] Crowe painted Byrne as a malicious busybody, who disliked Kirwan and this was confirmed by Caroline Bentley, a lifelong-friend of Sarah, who asserted that Byrne was in the habit of trying to turn Sarah against her husband, which eventually led her to sever the acquaintance.[21]

While Byrne may have been discredited, two other women who had been acquainted with Sarah during her stay in Howth also provided information to the crown, giving details of the Kirwans' domestic situation as revealed to them by Sarah herself which seemed to corroborate Byrne's evidence. A Mrs Gillas recounted how she was engaged as a washerwoman for the Kirwans and had almost daily contact with Sarah. She described how, a fortnight before her death, Sarah came to her house at five o'clock in the morning, 'very much fretted', wearing no stays and 'her hair hanging loose about', asking could she come in as her husband was after her.[22] Gillas revealed that Sarah told her that Kirwan 'was leading her a very bad life' and when questioned, confided that he had been beating her badly from soon after their marriage and she believed the cause of the violence was her lack of children.[23] Even more damning, Catherine Kelly, a Howth resident who had known Sarah as a fellow parishioner of Marlboro Street chapel, recounted how she had three visits from Sarah while staying in Howth, during which she described the abuse she had received at her husband's hands.[24] Five weeks before her death, Sarah arrived at Kelly's house limping and in tears and told Kelly that her husband 'who was treating her with great brutality' had beaten her with his walking stick the previous night. Kelly observed that Sarah's knees and legs were swollen and gave her some oil 'to rub to those pains and marks of violence'. A few days later, Sarah returned and revealed that although Kirwan was beating her badly, it was not as bad as before. On a third visit, three weeks before her death, Sarah divulged how she had received 'some heavy blows' and asked Kelly to accompany her to a local magistrate, Alderman Egan, to inform him of 'the brutal life she was leading from the ill treatment of her husband'. Kelly advised her to say nothing at that time, but to inform police on her return home. Sarah also told Kelly that Kirwan had another woman with whom he had had eight children and 'it must be on that woman's account he was beating her so badly'. Because of this, Kelly alleged that Sarah had asked Kirwan to separate, only requesting a small sum of money from him to live on, a request he refused, stating that he would give her no money as she was barren and would 'see you damned and very well hanged first'.

It is interesting to note that neither of these women appeared as witnesses in court and while both women were supportive of Sarah's situation and helped where they could, they seemed loath to get involved and attempted to underplay the situation. Gillas, having been told that the abuse was ongoing throughout the marriage, commented that 'the best will have words', while

Kelly, after Sarah's third visit, counselled her to 'bear it patiently'.[25] This attitude was not unusual at that time and Steiner-Scott notes that domestic violence was commonplace and widespread in 19th-century Ireland, and although daily newspaper reports detailed disturbing accounts of the abuse of women, there was little public condemnation.[26] Although the Offences against the Person Act of 1861 introduced aggravated assault as a charge and awarded tougher sentences for assault and battery of women,[27] in Irish domestic violence cases courts remained lenient. Caroline Conley observes that in post Famine Ireland, 70 per cent of men who were convicted of beating their wives to death were sentenced to 12 months or less.[28] Considered a petty crime, domestic violence was also seen as a private matter and police manuals of the day specifically directed the constabulary not to interfere too closely in domestic disputes.[29] The issue of whether the wife offered provocation for the abuse was a common theme, and courts tended to be particularly forgiving to husbands who used this defence, awarding light sentences or simply a fine.[30] Although beating one's wife was increasingly criticized from the 1820s onward, many women were reluctant to make their abuse public by prosecuting their husband in order to protect their children, their financial situation or their position in society.[31] Furthermore, there was a common belief that it was the wife's responsibility to try to ensure that the marriage succeeded rather than taking legal recourse.[32]

In the mid-19th century, Sarah Kirwan had little options available to her if her marriage was an unhappy one. Although unclear if she was aware of the existence of her husband's mistress, adultery by men (but not women) was widely accepted in law and public opinion in the mid-19th century.[33] A pamphlet defending Kirwan, although acknowledging his 'previous immoral life', urged readers not to judge him for his weakness.[34] This idea of male weakness echoes the prevailing belief that men were driven by desire, easily led astray and had little resistance to attractive women and can be seen in Theresa Kenny's statement, where she stated that 'the responsibility for my intimacy with Kirwan was mine not his'.[35] Another pamphlet lamented Kirwan's persecution by society because of his connection with Kenny, noting that a redeeming feature of his character was that he did not abandon his wife for his mistress and exhorted the public 'let the man who is without sin, cast the first stone'.[36]

Neither spousal violence nor male adultery were sufficient grounds for divorce in mid-19th-century Ireland. While a wife could prosecute a husband for cruelty in the courts, actual proof of physical violence was necessary and in a society where many considered a wife should submit to her husband's will, he could claim provocation as a defence. A wife was also believed to have no right to enquire into their husband's faithfulness.[37] Husbands had the right to sue their wives' lovers for damages in the civil law courts, known as criminal conversation, but there was no female equivalent.[38] Divorce was a lengthy process, culminating in a private act of parliament that dissolved the marriage, allowing the two parties to remarry. It was also expensive, with a suggested cost of £500 given by the Royal Commission on Divorce in the 1850s, an amount beyond the means of many, particularly for women who had no legal right to their own property, it being passed to her husband on marriage to use as he saw fit.[39]

Campaigns by Caroline Norton, herself a party in a criminal conversation case, detailed the injustices in the treatment of married women and sought legal reform of their rights regarding divorce, property and child custody.[40] Similarly, the feminist artist and women's activist, Barbara Leigh Smith, campaigned for more opportunities for all women, single, married, separated or widowed.[41] These campaigns would contribute to the enactment of the Divorce and Matrimonial Causes Act in 1857, which removed the need for an act of parliament and established a civil divorce court.[42] This law did not, however, apply to Ireland, and it did not include any provision for married women's rights to their property.[43] It would be 1870 before this issue was addressed in the Married Women's Property Act, which gave women the right to own and control their personal property.[44] It would be even later before marital cruelty was recognized by law in Ireland as grounds for divorce, following a private bill taken to parliament by Irishwoman Louisa Westropp, granddaughter of the earl of Mountcashel, in 1886 to divorce her husband on the grounds of his adultery and cruelty.[45] The first Irishwoman to present a divorce bill, this case set a precedent that domestic violence could be a valid reason for divorce, and following this case both adultery and marital cruelty became the most cited reasons for divorce by Irishwomen.[46]

If society was content to accept, or at least turn a blind eye to the dalliances of married men, attitudes towards those whom they consorted with, the so-called 'fallen women', were considerably harsher. Theresa Kenny described how, after exposure of her relationship with Kirwan, she was 'hunted and persecuted, almost driven to madness' and forced to move from lodging to lodging, whenever her identity was revealed.[47] On releasing a statement detailing these grievances, she was castigated by one newspaper for her 'self-degradation', and declared her 'deserving of deeper censure than ever fell before to woman'.[48] On her own evidence Kenny, then age 31, had known Kirwan since she was 7 years old, had been in a relationship with him for 14 years and could not recall if he had ever proposed marriage.[49] Kenny appears to be what McLoughlin calls a 'gentleman's miss', a woman of lower socio-economic class, whose relationship with a gentleman was a means to a comfortable life.[50] Their union could last some years or for life and the woman would usually have been provided with a small cottage and land for herself and her children, which would be legally deeded to her on the gentleman's death.[51] In this case, Kirwan's possessions were forfeit to the crown leaving Kenny without financial support and she reported that she received threats from the police that her children would be placed in the poorhouse, leading Boswell to petition the lord lieutenant for a public enquiry into their conduct.[52] As an unmarried mother of seven children Kenny would have been shunned and vilified by society, with little choices except to depend on her family for support, enter the workhouse system or resort to prostitution.[53] This vilification of unmarried mothers may account in part for the low rate of Irish illegitimate births, which in 1864, the first year official statistics on births were recorded, were just 3.8 per cent of total births, compared to 5 per cent in England.[54]

Kenny did attempt to make a claim on Kirwan's property in August 1853, stating that he had signed his lands in Longford over to her as a token of affection and as compensation for 'the injuries he had done her'.[55] In November of that same year these lands would also be the subject of an unsuccessful petition by Richard Downes-Bowyer's son Henry to be awarded their rental income, which he claimed were fraudulently obtained.[56] Kenny also claimed that Kirwan had paid her an allowance of £83 every six months and she was due one year of this payment.[57] However, her claim was dismissed as fraudulent and she was denounced by the court as a perjurer and a forger,[58] an opinion probably coloured by the notoriety she enjoyed as Kirwan's mistress. Kenny's misfortune was not to end there, as the solicitor engaged by her to represent her in this case was not all that he seemed. Mr George Balfour Darling had misrepresented himself to Kenny as a qualified solicitor, allowing him to obtain large sums of money from her, reported to be up to £10 as well as 'deeds and valuable documents'.[59] In consequence, and on Kenny's evidence, he was charged with 'obtaining money on false and fraudulent pretences'.[60] Darling, somewhat of a con artist, having three previous convictions for similar offences, was sentenced to four years' hard labour, which he would also spend in Spike Island.[61] Arriving on the island several months after Kirwan's departure for Bermuda, and released before his return, Darling fortunately avoided the man whose mistress he had defrauded.[62] Following this, Theresa Kenny and her children are said to have emigrated to America, possibly helped by the government due to her reduced financial circumstances and it was reported that on Kirwan's release he joined her there.[63] While this author is unable to locate any factual basis for this statement, Kirwan's prison record shows that he was 'released on licence 18 January 1879 and went to Queenstown', a port of emigration to North America.[64] Aged 63 on his release Kirwan was described as 'an aged and very respectable looking gentleman' who was 'white haired bent and feeble' and with nothing about his outward appearance to suggest him guilty of the crime he had committed.[65]

4. The law, transportation and imprisonment

'Bermuda, as the receptacle of our worst convicts'[1]

As well as calls for reform of the law regarding women's rights, a movement for reform of the law relating to criminal appeals had been ongoing since the 1840s and Kirwan's barrister Isaac Butt played a prominent role in this campaign.[2] At the time of Kirwan's conviction, the only right to appeal was on a point of law and this was at the discretion of the trial judge.[3] However, Kirwan's request for leave to appeal had been refused by Judge Crampton, the trial's presiding judge, following Butt's submission of legal objections.[4] The result of the case may have prompted Butt to attempt to further the campaign for a full court of criminal appeal and he introduced a bill in the house of commons in June 1853.[5] Mentioning the Kirwan case in his speech, he noted that as his sentence was commuted, there must have been some doubt as to his guilt and suggesting that rather than the current lingering doubt as to the correctness of the verdict, a system where a second appeal trial was available may have clarified Kirwan's guilt or innocence, and put an end to the public attention and controversy.[6] This sentiment was echoed by the newspapers, who noted that this case had shown the necessity for a court of criminal appeal where 'justice could have its protesting voice'.[7] The bill met with strong opposition, however, and a second reading was postponed.[8] Butt and his parliamentary colleagues would continue to introduce bills to establish a court of criminal appeal throughout the 19th century and by 1900 30 bills had been presented with still no prospect of reform.[9] It would be 1907 before a bill was passed that led to the setting up of a full court of criminal appeal in England and Wales although this did not apply to Ireland, where the Irish court of criminal appeal was not set up until 1924, after the formation of the Free State.[10]

Over 9,000 British and Irish convicts were sent to the Bermuda convict establishment between 1823 and 1863, employed in public works and building the Royal Naval Dockyard on Ireland Island. Conditions were grim and prisoners were housed in seven decommissioned Royal Navy ships known as prison hulks. Cold and damp in winter and boiling hot in summer the hulks were a breeding ground for many diseases such as consumption, bronchitis, dysentery, fever or opthalmia, an eye disease caused by the strong glare of the sun, and 1,260 of the 9,000 convicts died during their sentences from illness, accidents or suicide. Yellow Fever was a constant threat and there were three major epidemics during the colony's existence, in 1843, 1853 and 1856.[11] The notorious conditions were strongly criticized by the earl of Carnarvon, colonial

7. The convict dress at Bermuda, 17 June 1848 (© Illustrated London News Group, British Newspaper Archive, British Library)

under secretary, in 1860, who, quoting a report from a Bermuda chaplain, stated,

> Few are aware of the extent of suffering to which a prisoner is exposed on board the hulks, or the horrible nature of the associations by which he is surrounded. There is no safety for life, no supervision over the bad, no protection to the good. The hulks are unfit for a tropical climate. They are productive of sins of such foul impurity and unnatural crime that one even shudders to mention them.[12]

He demanded an enquiry into the situation with a view to abolishing the hulks. In fact, the situation was already in hand and from 1847 convicts were put to work building a new onshore prison in a part of the settlement called Boaz Island and by 1852 the hulks began to be taken out of service one by one and prisoners transferred to the prison.[13] However, in 1860, the earl of Carnarvon noted that two thirds of the 1,500 prisoners in Bermuda were still housed in the prison hulks.[14]

Petitions sent to the home office by Kirwan show that he was housed in the 'Tenedos' hulk in 1860 but by 1861[15] had been moved to Boaz Island and he appears to have been treated somewhat leniently, compared to other prisoners. An account by a British officer, in 1856, reported that Kirwan had never undergone hard labour being only ever assigned to light duties, working as a clerk in the hospital and this is reiterated by Charles Gibson, chaplain of Spike Island who related that because of this job his food rations were better than other prisoners.[16] Kirwan's notoriety gained him a high status with his fellow prisoners and Gibson notes that on his arrival another prisoner remarked 'before you came I held the first place in these islands, but I concede that honour to *Mr William Burke Kirwan*'.[17] In addition to the respect which he was given by fellow prisoners he was also 'allowed to cultivate his art (of painting)'.[18] This treatment is reminiscent of that of Irish patriot John Mitchel, himself a Protestant middle-class gentleman, who suggested that life as a convict in Bermuda for him was far from arduous as he was kept apart from other prisoners, assigned a servant and wore his own clothes.[19] With access to books and letters he noted that 'even as a felon the gentleman is not to mix with the swinish multitude'.[20] Kirwan's conduct was reported as very good and he was categorized as a 'special class' prisoner, stating in one of his petitions for early release that he had been this class 'during the whole term of his incarceration'.[21] This was the highest convict classification, awarded to most prisoners after promotion through the system from probation class on first imprisonment, and entitled Kirwan to extra remission, to write and receive letters more frequently than lower-class prisoners, to be appointed to positions of trust and receive an extra gratuity on discharge.[22]

While Kirwan may have been treated more favourably than other prisoners in Bermuda, this did not extend to his handling by the Irish administration. During one of the Yellow Fever epidemics in 1856, he had worked in the hospital as dispenser, nurse and night watchman and as a result gained the promise of two years remission from Sir George Lewis, the then-home secretary.[23] Following a recommendation from Charles Edwards, the prison's chief medical officer, for Kirwan's early release, based on his exceptional assistance during the epidemics, in 1858 Kirwan petitioned the lord lieutenant, the earl of Eglington, to be returned from Bermuda.[24] Eglington refused to recommend a reprieve for this 'dreadful murderer', stating that he felt at the time of Kirwan's conviction the death penalty should have been carried out and the denial of Kirwan's petition was a way of clearing himself for having commuted the sentence, an act he believed was wrong.[25] Kirwan sent a further petition in 1860, in his eighth year of imprisonment, requesting that the promise of remission be granted so he 'should have equal benefits with the other prisoners who acted in a similar capacity' and pleaded that he be allowed to go to America.[26] This was accompanied by letters of support from officers, chaplains, medical staff and overseers of the colony, ten staff in all, who praised his exemplary conduct and expressed their admiration and appreciation for his services during the epidemic.[27] This remission, however, was denied him by the Irish under secretary, Sir Thomas

IRELAND ISLAND, BERMUDA.—(FROM A SKETCH BY A CORRESPONDENT.)

8. Ireland Island, Bermuda, *Illustrated London News*, 17 June 1848 (© Illustrated London News Group, British Newspaper Archive, British Library)

Larcom, who stated that while Sir Lewis considered it admirable that Kirwan had gained the good opinion of the officers of the convict establishment, there would be no remission of his sentence on account of the 'circumstances of the heinous crime of which he was convicted'.[28] Larcom had been particularly keen to send Kirwan to either Bermuda or Gibraltar, both establishments where the arduous physical labour of quarrying stone meant that they were suited only to the youngest and fittest convicts.[29] A letter from the prisons office confirms this, requesting that the 246 convicts, including Kirwan, being transported aboard the *Amazon* to Bermuda be 'only prisoners physically fitted for hard labour in that climate'.[30] Kirwan sent four more petitions, up to 1863, continuing to plead for his promised remission, detailing his deteriorating health and eyesight because of the climate in Bermuda, excellent conduct and requesting to join his children in America. Isaac Butt, his defence solicitor, also attempted to gain mitigation of his sentence but to no avail.[31] The Irish administration consistently repeated their opposition to Kirwan's release and his return to Ireland, while denying his request to go to America as there was the possibility that he might return home from there.[32]

Under the penal transportation system, it had been general practice to grant early release to prisoners sentenced to transportation and convicts serving their sentences on hulks customarily had life sentences reduced to 10 years.[33] In cases where prisoners had been sentenced to death and had their sentences commuted to transportation to life, on completion of 12 years they could be eligible for remission or release with each case considered on its own merits.[34] By 1863, Kirwan, with the remission that was promised to him, had completed over and above this sentence, a fact pointed out in a letter to Earl Grey from the Bermuda administration.[35] A note on his prison file from 1862 does mention the possibility of a conditional pardon, at that stage of his imprisonment (which would prevent him returning to Ireland), but goes on to state that 'if he is really guilty the term for that has hardly arrived'.[36] On the break-up of the Bermuda convict establishment in 1863, many of the remaining convicts were transferred to Western Australia.[37] Kirwan, however was transferred to Millbank penitentiary in London, arriving on 11 April 1863, sending a further petition for clemency from there, where he pleaded for conditional release, known as a ticket of leave, to Canada, noting that he had undergone over the usual term of life sentence needed to obtain this.[38] On this matter, though, the Irish administration were intransigent, claiming that remission was 'particularly objectionable', that they could not agree to his liberation and saw no reason to reverse their earlier stance.[39] Larcom lamented that it was unfortunate that 'some mode of disposing of this convict could not have been found, other than return him to Ireland', while a notation attached to this letter stated 'they may keep him in prison as long as they please'.[40] Their wishes were not adhered to and following a request from the under secretary to receive him, Kirwan was transferred from Millbank back to Spike Island in May 1863, where he remained until his release in 1879.[41] On his return to Ireland, Kirwan appears to have accepted his fate as there were no more petitions sent for the remainder of his prison term.

A note in the papers of Thomas Larcom may, in part, explain his uncompromising stance towards Kirwan's release. In 1842, during his tenure as Irish director of the Ordnance Survey, one of his surveyors, Alfred Byrne, was killed near Milltown in Dublin in mysterious circumstances.[42] Byrne, by coincidence a neighbour of Kirwan's, living at 8 Parnell Place, was found dead in a lime kiln with his throat cut but, amid suggestions of suicide and suspicion falling upon his brother, following a four-day inquest, the jury were unable to clarify the circumstances of his death.[43] Larcom, who took a personal interest in the case, retained a newspaper report of the inquest on which he wrote, obviously at a later date, that he had 'no doubt that this was one of the several concealed murders committed by Kirwan'.[44] This, he maintained was due to the similar mysterious circumstances surrounding both Byrne and Sarah Kirwan's death, both of which 'baffled enquiry' and 'defied the Coroner'.[45] Furthermore, it is also possible, that Larcom was personally acquainted with Kirwan, through his work as a colourist of maps for the Ordnance Survey.[46]

5. Victorian moral codes and newspaper reporting

'A newspaper controversy and a topic of earnest gossip about town'.[1]

The Irish middle classes in the 19th century tended to turn a blind eye to marital disharmony, to uphold their values of domesticity, respectability and morality. Kirwan, however, exposed as an unfaithful husband and father of illegitimate children had transgressed these values. The opening remarks of the prosecution that 'affection and kind regard on the part of the husband have not gone hand in hand with duty' and of his connection of an 'illicit and immoral character with another woman'[2] set the tone for the trial. Kirwan's defence team attempted to mitigate this and Butt asked the jury to disregard Kirwan's infidelity, which he stated was the reason for his prosecution and a crime he had paid for already with humiliation and imprisonment.[3] This infidelity was seized upon by the newspapers and reports of Kirwan's crime and lifestyle exude moral outrage, describing his 'hardly disguised and habitual adultery' and his 'career of hidden iniquity'.[4] This type of moral commentary was common in Victorian newspapers and through the press, transgressions against societal values were spread nationwide, transforming them into causes célèbres.[5]

Kirwan was decried as a 'libertine', 'a monster in human form' and a 'heartless seducer' by the Catholic nationalist press.[6] In contrast, Protestant newspapers took a softer line, describing Kirwan as 'wretched', suggesting that Kirwan may be 'penitent for the crimes and errors of his past life' and that his connection with his 'paramour' was not an adequate motive for such a heinous murder, while condemning the nationalist press for 'hounding the unfortunate man to his death'.[7] Notwithstanding this, as the controversy continued, newspapers from both sides of the religious divide related any salacious detail of Kirwan's life that could be found, proven or not. The police were reported by the *Belfast Newsletter* to be 'very active' in investigating a series of 'terrible crimes' that Kirwan was alleged to have been responsible for, although the newspaper did admit that 'many of these reports were completely groundless'.[8] He was denounced as an art forger, for non payment of debts, and for the seduction of a servant girl.[9] The 1839 allegation of seduction of a girl of a respectable family resurfaced, with more details revealed of the events leading up to and following the court proceedings. It was claimed that he had lived with this woman in Holyhead for a short time, before leaving her in a destitute state, which resulted in ill health from which she never recovered.[10] In addition, not content with posting placards around Dublin denouncing Kirwan's behaviour, her brother was reported to have horsewhipped him severely which led to another prosecution by Kirwan.

However, his assailant was not convicted as the court considered itself satisfied that justice had been done in this case.[11]

Anne Bowyer, wife of Kirwan's mentor, Richard Downes Bowyer, also made a reappearance, repeating her accusation from 1837, that Kirwan had murdered her husband for his money and property.[12] Since that time, Bowyer had continued to seek her husband, advertising in the press in 1843 for any information relating to his whereabouts.[13] Reported in great detail by the newspapers, Bowyer's accusation was taken seriously by the police who dug up the garden of Kirwan's former lodgings in Harold's Cross in search of a body. Although the decayed remains of a coffin and the bones of a small child were excavated, it was concluded that they had been in the ground for many years and had no bearing on the present case.[14] The allegation was subsequently proven false by the ever-reliable Knight Boswell, who produced another pamphlet detailing the circumstances of Richard Downes Boyer's disappearance.[15] According to Boswell, Anne Bowyer could be mentally unstable and was sometimes violent towards her husband, leading to their separation in 1836, which Downes Bowyer registered in court, agreeing that an annual annuity would be paid to his wife. Anne, however, sought to break the agreement and resume the marriage and took to following Bowyer to the various lodgings he procured in Dublin until he eventually sought refuge in Killeshandra, Co. Cavan, where he lived under an assumed name. He died aged 79 in 1841 and Boswell produced a copy of the Killeshandra parish register, furnished by its rector, recording his burial.[16] Anne Bowyer herself would die in July 1853 in questionable circumstances, found drowned in a quarry hole, her clothing found folded nearby and an inquest heard that since Kirwan's conviction she had become overly preoccupied by his alleged theft of her husband's property.[17] Also in this pamphlet Knight Boswell refuted another allegation against Kirwan, that of the murder of Sarah's brother, a charge first levelled by Maria Byrne in her evidence to the crown but contradicted emphatically by Maria Crowe, his mother, who produced a letter sent from his home in Massachusetts to his sister before her death.[18]

The stream of stories such as these led Boswell to protest that Kirwan was being charged and tried by the public press and one newspaper described Kirwan as 'a very maligned individual'.[19] However, a fascination with murder and violent crime among the middle and lower classes ensured that crime reporting was an extremely popular feature of British newspapers in the 19th century, growing in popularity as the century progressed.[20] Public interest in sensationalized reports of violent crime saw newspapers increase their coverage to meet the demand and to gain wider readership, and this wide coverage of shocking and scandalous crimes was a particular feature of the Victorian era. Often criticized for reporting crime in a particularly emotive and lurid fashion, crime journalists of the day, when facts were unavailable, relied on speculation and exaggeration.[21] The language used to describe murder in Irish newspapers

9. Engraving of tourists visiting the Long Hole, a recommended Howth attraction even in 1866. Sir Cusack P. Roney, *How to spend a month in Ireland* (London, 1866), p. 10.

was vivid and designed to both shock and draw the reader's attention with murders invariably reported using such words such as 'revolting', 'savage', 'barbarous', 'atrocious' or 'dreadful'.[22] Despite the extensive Irish reportage of all aspects of the Kirwan trial and its aftermath, they seemed determined to deny this fascination with the case and violent crime in general, deeming it an English phenomenon. When reporting that the rock on Ireland's Eye that Sarah Kirwan's body was found had disappeared, having been carried away in fragments by tourists to the site, these visitors were described as English.[23] The immorality of Kirwan's crime was also described by some Irish newspapers as 'a purely English one' and a barbarity that belonged with the 'horrors which give England the bloody reputation for immorality and crime'.[24] As Carolyn Conley contends, a prevalent belief in late-19th-century Ireland was that while homicide might be caused by alcohol, passion or as the result of a brawl, actual murder with intent was considered un-Irish.[25] A case in point was an article in the nationalist *Ulsterman,* which insisted that it was the unparalleled nature of the Kirwan murder that ensured its notoriety in Ireland as there had never been 'the fearful atrocities that load the criminal records in England'.[26]

Certainly, women accounted for only 8 per cent of murder victims between 1842 and 1846 and the majority of all murders were as a result of brawls, arguments or family disputes, coming from fairs or in public houses.[27] After the mid-century, murder cases involving middle- or upper-class defendants were rare, but when convicted they could expect a higher sentence as their respectability, a trait marked by the ability to control natural urges, should have allowed them to contain their violent impulses.[28] Conley also notes that at that time murders of wives during a beating or as a result of a drunken quarrel were treated leniently by the courts but premeditated murder of a spouse was considered so heinous the accused was likely to be considered insane or receive the death penalty.[29] A perusal of newspaper reports from 1850 to 1853 appears to confirm this. Martin Gannon, a shopkeeper from Roscrea, James Crowley, a carpet cutter from Dublin, Patrick Flanagan of Derry and William McCready, described as a 'comfortable farmer', all of whose wives died as a result of a beating from their husbands were all acquitted of murder and convicted of manslaughter.[30] Catherine Moran from Ardnaree was admitted to hospital with severe injuries, dying shortly afterwards, and although she stated they were caused by a violent kicking by her husband (who had absconded), the coroner's inquest found that she had died from an injury inflicted by 'some person unknown'.[31] A Dr Langley of Nenagh, charged with murdering his wife by depriving her of food and medicine and imprisoning her in a cold room, was found not guilty.[32] In contrast, Patrick Monaghan who strangled his wife in Mayo, and Denis Haly, found guilty of attempting to poison his wife, were both executed.[33] None of these murders elicited the press coverage that was given to the Kirwan case. Kirwan's class, his lifestyle and the nature of the murder ensured his notoriety and the fascination with this case continued throughout his imprisonment.[34]

Conclusion

The Kirwan murder case and the social commentary that followed affords a fascinating insight into Dublin middle-class life of the mid-19th century. Kirwan, as part of Dublin's Protestant professional class, was a member of the social hierarchy of the city and would have benefited from the privileged nature of this position. His rank may have contributed to the shock value of his arrest and conviction when murder was rare and the majority committed were after brawls or quarrels and fuelled by alcohol. Premeditated murder of a spouse was considered particularly heinous, when most of the wife murders of the time resulted from a beating or a drunken fight. The revelation of his illicit liaison and the resulting seven children added to the scandal and Kirwan was denounced as much for this 'crime' as he was for the murder of his wife Sarah.

The case allows a glimpse of different aspects of Dublin and Irish middle-class society. The Dublin school of medicine of the early 19th century and their pioneering work in medical teaching and practice gained a worldwide reputation and contributed to the position of these physicians and surgeons as society's elite. Kirwan's links to these senior medical professionals and their support for him, even after his conviction, indicate that he was part of this privileged and influential world. The employment of Isaac Butt, eminent barrister and MP, reflects Kirwan's affluence and reinforces this status. The nature of the trial evidence, the ambiguousness of the verdict and Kirwan's lack of options for appeal after the guilty verdict reflects the need at that time for the establishment of a full court of criminal appeal. The controversial nature of the case allowed it to be used as a specific example of this need throughout the campaign for a full court. Also, regarding the need for legal reform, the lack of legal rights available to Sarah Kirwan as a possible victim of domestic violence and the apparent toleration of this violence by the courts reflects the gendered nature of the law at that time.

The prison and penal transportation system, particularly the treatment of prisoners when this method of punishment was coming to its end is also well represented. Kirwan's apparent preferential treatment in prison and in the convict settlement of Bermuda shows that even in the penal system, society was stratified by class. Class, however, did not mitigate his treatment by the Irish administration and despite other prisoners customarily gaining remission in similar cases to Kirwan's, he was not afforded this. It is possible that Kirwan's notoriety and the controversy the case generated was not to his advantage in his quest for remission, as his release would have resulted in further outcry, something the administration would wish to avoid.

The case also provides a view of some of the attitudes held by middle-class Irish society. Sectarian divisions appeared after the verdict, propagated by newspaper reporting, despite evidence that they did not impact the Kirwans' life as a couple in a mixed marriage. From contemporary literature on the case, it is noticeable Sarah Kirwan and Theresa Kenny appear to have almost become a footnote, eclipsed by the notoriety of their husband and lover, reflecting women's status in society and its patriarchal nature. Societal discourses around motherhood are represented by Sarah Kirwan's intake of what are now considered toxic chemicals and her practice of sea-bathing, in what may have been an attempt to 'cure' her possible infertility. They are also shown in the suggestion that she may have accepted Kenny, who gave her husband seven children, because of this infertility. However, after Kirwan's conviction, society did not accept Kenny and her treatment as a 'fallen' woman shows the societal 'double standard', where sexual purity for women and sexual freedom for men were widely accepted, despite prevailing middle-class values of domesticity, gentility and morality. Newspapers, particularly the Catholic press, castigated Kirwan for contravening these values, declaring his crime particularly un-Irish, possibly referring to Kirwan's Protestant religion, underlining societal sectarian division. However, their avowed distaste for the crime did not limit their extensive coverage of this case to meet the demand of a public fascinated by violent crime.

Notes

ABBREVIATIONS

AC	*Anglo Celt*
BNL	*Belfast News-Letter*
CC	*Cork Constitution*
CE	*Cork Examiner*
CJEA	*Clare Journal and Ennis Advertiser*
CSORP	Chief Secretary's Office Registered Papers
CSR	*Cork Southern Reporter*
CT	*Connaught Telegraph*
DEM	*Dublin Evening Mail*
DEP	*Dublin Evening Post*
DEPC	*Dublin Evening Packet and Correspondent*
DIB	James McGuire & James Quinn (eds), *Dictionary of Irish biography*, 9 vols (Cambridge, 2009)
DMA	*Dublin Morning Advertiser and Weekly Price Current*
DMR	*Dublin Morning Register*
DN	*Daily News*
DWN	*Dublin Weekly Nation*
EF	*Evening Freeman*
FJ	*Freeman's Journal*
GPO	General Prisons Office
IE	*Irish Examiner*
LCE	*Limerick and Clare Examiner*
LDN	*London Evening Standard*
LWN	*Lloyds Weekly Newspaper*
MA	*Morning Advertiser*
MLA	*Meath and Louth Advertiser*
NAI	National Archives of Ireland
NELA	*Newry Examiner and Louth Advertiser*
NG	*Nenagh Guardian*
NLI	National Library of Ireland
NYT	*New York Times*
OSI	Ordnance Survey of Ireland
SC	*Sligo Champion*
SNL	*Saunders' News-Letter*
SRCCC	*Southern Reporter and Cork Commercial Courier*
TC	*Tyrone Constitution*
TN	*Nation*
TNA	The National Archives (London)
UM	*Ulsterman*
WFJ	*Weekly Freeman's Journal*
WM	*Waterford Mail*

INTRODUCTION

1 Walter G. Strickland, *A dictionary of Irish artists* (Dublin, 1913), p. 596.

2 J.S. Armstrong, *Report of the trial of William Burke Kirwan, for the murder of Maria Louisa Kirwan, his wife, at the island of Ireland's Eye, in the county of Dublin, on the 6th September, 1852, before the Hon. Judge Crampton and the Rt. Hon. Baron Green, at the Commission Court, Green-street, on 8th and 9th December 1852* (Dublin, 1853), p. 91.

3 Michael Sheridan, *Murder at Ireland's Eye* (Dublin, 2012), p. 33; Armstrong, *Report of the trial of William Burke Kirwan*, p. 4; for example, 'The Murderer's Christmas', *IE*, 29 Dec. 1852.

4 *CE*, 17 Jan. 1853; *LDN*, 9 Jan. 1853; for example, An Observer, 'The case of William Bourke Kirwan', *The Times* [of London], 16 Dec. 1852; A Barrister, 'The case of William Bourke Kirwan', ibid., 23 Dec. 1852.

5 John Knight Boswell, *Defence of William Bourke Kirwan, condemned for the alleged murder of his wife, and now a convict in Spike Island to which, amongst other documents, is appended the opinion of Alfred S. Taylor, M.D., F.R.S. the most eminent medico-legal writer in the Empire, that 'no murder was committed'* (Dublin, 1853); Thomas Geoghegan, *An examination of the medical facts in the case of the Queen v W.B. Kirwan* (Dublin, 1853); Samuel Haughton, *On the true height of the tide at Ireland's Eye on the evening of the 6th September, 1852, the day of the murder of Mrs Kirwan* (Dublin, 1861); Revd Malet, *The Kirwan case illustrating the danger of conviction on circumstantial evidence, and the necessity of granting new trials in criminal cases* (Dublin, 1853).

6 *CT*, 5 Jan. 1853; Irish Prison Registers 1790–1924, William Burke Kirwan, Mountjoy Prison Convict Classification 1857–1866, NAI, 1/11/23/1.

7 Matthias McDonnell Bodkin, *Famous Irish trials* (Dublin, 1918); William Roughead, 'The secret of Ireland's Eye: a detective story' in idem, *The fatal countess and other studies* (Edinburgh, 1924); Sheridan, *Murder at Ireland's Eye*; W.E. Vaughan, *Murder trials in Ireland, 1836–1914* (Dublin, 2009).

8 Brendan Nolan, *Dublin folk tales* (Dublin, 2012).

9 Vincent Mc Brierty, *The Howth peninsula: its history, lore and legend* (Dublin, 1982).

I. THE KIRWAN MURDER, CASE AND TRIAL

1 Armstrong, *Report of the trial of William Burke Kirwan*, p. 2.

2 Sheridan, *Murder at Ireland's Eye*, pp 14–15.

3 Ibid., p. 16.

4 *Thom's Irish almanac and official directory with the post office Dublin city and county directory for the year 1852* (Dublin, 1852), p. 925.

5 'Letters of John Rennie, and John Rennie Jnr, Engineers on the building of Howth Harbour', *Dublin Historical Record*, 61:1 (Spring, 2008), 2–4.

6 *Thom's Irish almanac 1852*, p. 925; *FJ*, 7 June 1847.

7 Armstrong, *Report of the trial of William Burke Kirwan*, p. 14.

8 *DWN*, 22 May 1847; *FJ*, 7 June 1847; ibid., 27 June 1851.

9 Thomas E. Jordan, 'The quality of life in Victorian Ireland, 1831–1901', *New Hibernia Review*, 4:1 (2000), 103–21; *FJ*, 22 May 1847.

10 *TN*, 17 July 1847; *FJ*, 16 July 1847.

11 *Thom's Irish almanac 1852*, p. 925.

12 Sheridan, *Murder at Ireland's Eye*, p. 14; Mr and Mrs S.C. Hall, *Ireland: its scenery, character etc*, vol. 2 (London, 1842), pp 291–3; James Fraser, *A hand book for travellers in Ireland* (Dublin, 1844), p. 664.

13 Mc Brierty, *The Howth peninsula*.

14 Malet, *The Kirwan case*, p. 91.

15 Brief on behalf of the Crown in the case of the Queen v. William Burke Kirwan, trial for the murder of Maria L. Kirwan on Ireland's Eye, NAI, M.3074/1852.

16 Armstrong, *Report of the trial of William Burke Kirwan*, pp 6–8.

17 Ibid.

18 'Melancholy death by drowning', *DEM*, 8 Sept. 1852.

19 Sheridan, *Murder at Ireland's Eye*, p. 30.

20 Ibid., pp 31–4.

21 Statement of Maria Byrne, NAI, M.3074/1852/91.

22 Armstrong, *Report of the trial of William Burke Kirwan*, pp 18–19.

23 Ibid., p. 29.

24 NAI, M.3074/1852.

25 *IE*, 11 Oct. 1852.

26 Armstrong, *Report of the trial of William Burke Kirwan*, pp 27–8.

27 Bodkin, *Famous Irish trials*, p. 108; 'Second declaration of Theresa Kenny', *Morning Post*, 31 Jan. 1853.

28 *IE*, 11 Oct. 1852.

29 *FJ*, 9 Oct. 1852.

30 *BNL*, 29 Oct. 1852.

31 'An extraordinary charge of murder', *BNL*, 10 Dec. 1852.

32 *FJ*, 11 Dec. 1852; *SC*, 20 Dec. 1852.

33 Armstrong, *Report of the trial of William Burke Kirwan*, p. 91; *DEM*, 13 Dec. 1852.

34 *NELA*, 15 Dec. 1852.

35 Carolyn Conley, *Melancholy accidents: the meaning of violence in post-Famine Ireland* (Oxford, 1999), p. 215.

36 Vaughan, *Murder trials in Ireland*, p. 22; pp 388–9.

37 *Tables of number of criminal offenders committed for trial, or bailed for appearances at the assizes and sessions in each count, 1852; with the result of the proceedings* (1654), HC 1852–3, lxxxi, 433, p. 90.

38 'The Ireland's Eye murder', *NYT*, 15 Jan. 1853; *Sydney Freeman's Journal*, 21 May 1853; *Inquirer (Perth)*, 3 Aug. 1853.

39 *IE*, 29 Dec. 1852; Armstrong, *Report of the trial of William Burke Kirwan*, p. 4.

40 *Thom's Irish almanac 1852*, p. 441; Armstrong, *Report of the trial of William Burke Kirwan*, pp 36–7.

41 Philip Bull, 'Butt, Isaac', in DIB; Armstrong, *Report of the trial of William Burke Kirwan*, p. 47.

42 *FJ*, 27 July 1844; Malet, *The Kirwan case*, p. 91.

43 *CE*, 19 Jan. 1853; An Observer, 'The case of William Bourke Kirwan', *The Times* [of London], 16 Dec. 1852; A Barrister, 'The case of William Bourke Kirwan', *The Times*, 23 Dec. 1852; The case of Mr Kirwan', *LDN*, 31 Dec. 1852.

44 Malet, *The Kirwan case*; Boswell, *Defence of William Bourke Kirwan*.

45 Geoghegan, *An examination of the medical facts*.

46 Charles Benson and Siobhan Fitzpatrick, 'Pamphlets' in James Murphy (ed.), *The Oxford history of the Irish book, iv: the Irish book in English, 1800–1891* (Oxford, 2011), pp 139–43.

47 TNA, H018/349/1852; *CE*, 17 Jan. 1853; *LWN*, 9 Jan. 1853.

48 Copy of the resolutions agreed to at a numerous meeting at Anderson's Hotel the 10 Jan. 1853; Subsequent refusal noted on reverse 18 Apr. 1853, TNA, HO18/349/1852.

49 TNA, HO18/349/1852.

50 Mr I. Butt, House of Commons, 1 Jun. 1853 in *Hansard* 3, i [etc.] *Hansard's parliamentary debates*, 3rd series, 1830–91 (vols i–ccclvi, London, 1831–91); *MA*, 20 Dec. 1852.

51 *SNL*, 8 Jan. 1853; *FJ*, 20 Jan. 1853.

52 Note regarding foreman of the coroner's jury, 21 Mar. 1853, TNA, HO18/349/1852.

53 *EF*, 1 Jan. 1853.

54 *IE*, 28 Jan. 1853; *FJ*, 3 Jan. 1853.

55 Ibid., 27 Jan. 1853.

56 Richard MacMahon, '"Let the law take its course": Punishment and the exercise of the prerogative of mercy in pre-Famine and Famine Ireland' in Michael Brown and Sean Patrick Donlan (eds), *The laws and other legalities in Ireland, 1689–1850* (Surrey, 1988), p. 137.

57 Ibid., p. 153.

58 Motion for Correspondence, earl of Eglinton, 13 June 1861 in *Hansard* 3, I [etc.] *Hansard's parliamentary debates*, 3rd series, 1830–91 (vols i–ccvi, London, 1831–91).

59 *FJ*, 13 Dec. 1852; *DEM*, 15 Dec. 1852.

60 *DEP*, 18 Jan. 1853.

61 *IE*, 2 Feb. 1853.

62 *FJ*, 11 Jan. 1853; 'An island purgatory' available at Spike Island, Cork Harbour (http://www.spikeislandcork.Irish Examiner/history/island-purgatory) (accessed 4 Dec. 2015).

63 *FJ*, 20 Jan. 1853.

64 Cal McCarthy and Barra Ó Donnabháin, *Too beautiful for thieves and pickpockets: a history of the Victorian convict prison on Spike Island* (Cork, 2016), p. 15.

65 Charles Bernard Gibson, *Life among convicts* (London, 1863), p. 150.

66 Charles Bernard Gibson, *Irish convict reform, the intermediate prisons, a mistake, by an Irish prison chaplain in the convict service* (Dublin, 1863), pp 20–1.

67 McCarthy and Ó Donnabháin, *Too beautiful*, p. 229.

68 Ibid.

69 *IE*, 19 Jan. 1953; 'Answers to
    correspondents' in *TN*, 2 July 1853; 'The
    poor and the rich in prison', *FJ*, 25 July
    1853; *LCE*, 19 Jan. 1853.
70 *NELA*, 11 June 1853.
71 *IE*, 19 Jan. 1853.
72 *DEP*, 20 Jan. 1853.
73 *EF*, 25 July 1853.
74 McCarthy and Ó Donnabháin, *Too
    beautiful*, p. 108; William Burke Kirwan,
    Petitions to Sir George Grey, Colonial
    Secretary, 29 Apr. 1860, 4 Dec. 1861,
    23 Dec. 1862, 15 Apr. 1863, TNA,
    HO18/349/1852; William Burke Kirwan,
    Petition to Sir George Grey, 29 Apr. 1860,
    TNA, HO18/349/1852; NAI, 1/11/23/1.
75 Attested list of inmates, Boaz Island
    Prison, quarter ended 31 Mar. 1863,
    TNA, HO8/155/1852; England &
    Wales, Crime, prisons & punishment,
    1770–1935, Millbank Prison, Middlesex:
    register of prisoners, TNA, PCOM2/47.
76 NAI, 1/11/23/1; McCarthy and Ó
    Donnabháin, *Too beautiful*, pp 325–34.

2. THE KIRWANS' LIFE IN DUBLIN

1   Armstrong, *Report of the trial of William
    Burke Kirwan*, p. 41.
2   NAI, 1/11/23/1; Index to the act or
    grant books, and to original wills, of the
    Diocese of Dublin 1272–1858 (26th, 30th
    and 31st Reports of the Deputy Keeper
    of the Public Records of Ireland, 1894,
    1899).
3   Strickland, *Dictionary of Irish artists*,
    p. 596; *DMA*, 14 Jan. 1853.
4   *DEP*, 20 Aug. 1839; Strickland,
    Dictionary of Irish artists, p. 596.
5   Ibid.
6   *DEPC*, 21 May 1842.
7   Strickland, *Dictionary of Irish artists*, pp
    85–6.
8   Mary Forrest, 'Nurseries and
    nurserymen in Ireland from the early
    eighteenth to the early twenty-first
    century', *Studies in the History of Gardens
    & Designed Landscapes*, 30:4 (2010),
    323–66; Griffith's valuation of Ireland
    (Primary valuation of tenements),
    1847–1864, parish of Donnybrook, p. 35.
9   Statement of Thomas Brigford, NAI,
    M.3074/1852/85.

10 W.B. Kirwan Collection, NLI,
    PD2085TX (17); *EF*, 29 May 1845.
11 *CE*, 12 Jan. 1853; Frank Cullen, *Dublin
    1847: city of the ordnance survey* (Dublin,
    2015), pp 3–4.
12 Strickland, *Dictionary of Irish artists*,
    p. 240; David Cooper, 'Petrie, George' in
    DIB.
13 *CE*, 12 Jan. 1853; Cullen, *Dublin 1847*, p. 3.
14 NLI, PD2085TX (15); Cullen, *Dublin
    1847*, p. 4.
15 Armstrong, *Report of the trial of William
    Burke Kirwan*, p. 4.
16 *SNL*, 16 Aug. 1839.
17 James Kelly, 'The decline of duelling
    and the emergence of the middle class
    in Ireland' in Fintan Lane (ed.), *Politics,
    society and the middle class in Ireland*
    (Basingstoke, 2010), pp 86–102.
18 *SNL*, 16 Aug. 1839.
19 Ibid.
20 *DEM*, 26 Oct. 1840.
21 *FJ*, 27 May 1837.
22 'Ordnance Survey Ireland (OSI) 19th
    century historical maps', held by
    Ordnance Survey Ireland. © Public
    domain. Digital content: © Ordnance
    Survey Ireland, published by
    UCD Library, University College
    Dublin (http://digital.ucd.ie/view/
    ucdlib:40377).
23 *Dublin almanac and general register of
    Ireland, 1843* (Dublin, 1843), p. 641;
    *Dublin almanac and general register of
    Ireland, 1844* (Dublin, 1844), p. 825;
    Statement of Mr. Kelly, NAI, M.3074/
    1852/92; *Dublin almanac and general register
    of Ireland* (Dublin, 1847), p. 767; *Thom's
    Irish almanac and official directory with the
    post office Dublin city and county for the year
    1851* (Dublin, 1851), pp 768–9.
24 Ibid.
25 *BNL*, 20 Oct. 1852; Griffith's valuation,
    Trinity Ward, p. 85; *Thom's Irish almanac
    1851*, pp 768–9.
26 *FJ*, 15 Sept. 1853; 28 Sept. 1853.
27 'County of Longford and City of
    Dublin. In the matter of the goods and
    so forth of William Burke Kirwan, a
    felon', *FJ*, 21 Nov. 1853.
28 William Kemmis, Crown Solicitor
    to Thomas Larcom, Under Secretary
    for Ireland, 30 Nov. 1853, TNA,
    HO18/349/1852; *AC*, 1 Dec. 1853.

29 Armstrong, *Report of the trial of William Burke Kirwan*, p. 4.

30 *BNL*, 15 Dec. 1852; Jordan, 'Quality of life in Victorian Ireland'.

31 Bodkin, *Famous Irish trials*, p. 108; Boswell, *Defence of William Bourke Kirwan*, pp 34–6.

32 Wm B. Kirwan, 1848, The William Smith O'Brien Petition 1848–49, NAI, CRF/1848/O/16/2/051 pt. 2; Richard P. Davis, 'O'Brien, William Smith' in DIB.

33 'Ordnance Survey Ireland (OSI) 19th Century Historical Maps,' (http://digital.ucd.ie/view/ucdlib:40377).

34 *BNL*, 10 Sept. 1852; *AC*, 9 Sept. 1852; *BNL*, 10 Sept. 1852; *TN*, 11 Sept. 1852; Services of Officers (retired) on full and half pay, returns to the circular letter of 22 Oct 1828, p. 367, TNA, WO25/754.

35 *SNL*, 18 Mar. 1820; Lieutenant James Crowe, *Correspondence with several noble, dignified, and eminent persons furnishing testimonials of character and conduct with other documentary proofs* (Dublin, 1835), p. 13; *Dublin almanac and general register of Ireland* (Dublin, 1840), p. 604.

36 *MLA*, 1 Mar. 1823; Douglas W. Allen, 'Compatible incentives and the purchase of military commissions', *Journal of Legal Studies*, 27:1 (1998) 45–6; TNA, WO25/754; *London Gazette*, 21 June 1813; *Edinburgh Gazette*, 25–6 June 1816; TNA, WO25/754; Jamaica family search genealogy research library, The Jamaica almanac, 1817, 2nd West India regiment (www.jamaicanfamilysearch.com/Members/AL1817_05.htm) (accessed 10 Jan. 2017).

37 Desmond Bowen & Jan Bowen, *Heroic option: the Irish in the British Army* (Barnsley, 2005), pp 23–4; James Karsten, 'Irish soldiers in the British Army, 1792–1922: suborned or subordinate', *Journal of Social History*, 17:1 (Autumn, 1983), 31–44.

38 Ibid.; Richard Keogh and James McConnel, 'The Esmond family of Co. Wexford and catholic loyalty' in Oliver P. Rafferty (ed.), *Irish Catholic identities* (Manchester, 2013), pp 281–2.

39 *London Gazette*, 21 June 1813; Keogh and Mc Connel, 'The Esmond family', p. 281.

40 Allen, 'Compatible incentives', 50.

41 *MLA*, 1 Mar. 1823.

42 *FJ*, 3 Sept. 1819; Gerard Ó Tuathaigh, 'Daniel O'Connell' in *DIB*; John O'Connell (ed.), *The life and speeches of Daniel O'Connell MP* (Dublin, 1846), pp 382–3; Ó Tuathaigh, 'Daniel O'Connell'.

43 File of papers relating to Lieutenant James Crowe, NAI, CSO/RP/1821/1022.

44 Letter from J. Crowe, Dublin, renewing request for government employment, NAI, CSO/RP/1821/1530.

45 O'Connell, *Life and speeches of Daniel O'Connell*, pp 382–3.

46 Crowe, *Correspondence*.

47 Ibid.

48 British War Office, *A list of the officers of the army and of the Corps of Royal Marines on full, retired or half pay with an index* (London, 1833), p. 504.

49 British Army Pension Records, Records Information Leaflet No. 123, TNA, June 1997, (http://hewat.net/hewat/ri123.htm) (accessed 6 Jan. 2017).

50 TNA, WO25/754; Allen, 'Compatible incentives', 46.

51 Crowe, *Correspondence*, p. 2.

52 Thomas Willis, *The hidden Dublin: facts connected with the social and sanitary condition of the working classes in the city of Dublin* (Dublin, 1845), p. 44.

53 David Dickson, *Dublin: the making of a capital city* (Dublin, 2014), p.375; Willis, *Hidden Dublin*, pp 44–5.

54 Willis, *Hidden Dublin*, pp 44–5.

55 *Dublin almanac and general register of Ireland, 1840* (Dublin 1840), p. 598; Maria Luddy, *Prostitution and Irish society, 1800–1940* (Cambridge, 2007), p. 28.

56 'Ordnance Survey Ireland (OSI) 19th Century Historical Maps,' (http://digital.ucd.ie/view/ucdlib:40377).

57 Cullen, *Dublin 1847*, p. 63, p.73; Dickson, *Dublin*, p. 372.

58 Malet, *The Kirwan case*, pp 90–2; *DEM*, 26 Oct. 1840.

59 Joan Perkins, *Women and marriage in nineteenth-century England* (London, 1989), pp 21–2.

60 Raymond Lee, 'Intermarriage, conflict and social control in Ireland: the Decree 'Ne temere'', *Economic and Social Review*, 17:1 (1985), 11–27.

61 Ibid.

62 Malet, *The Kirwan case*, pp 90–2.

63 Donald Akenson, *Small differences: Irish Catholics and Irish Protestants, 1815–1922: an international perspective* (Dublin, 1991), pp 111–14.

64 Lee, 'Intermarriage, conflict and social control', 15.

65 Akenson, *Small differences*, p. 113.

66 Malet, *The Kirwan case*, pp 90–2.

67 Statement of Nicholas Kenny, NAI, M.3091/1852/83.

68 Armstrong, *Report of the trial of William Burke Kirwan*, pp 4–5; Boswell, *Defence of William Bourke Kirwan*, pp 34–6.

69 Malet, *The Kirwan case*, pp 93–5; Statement of Mr Kelly, NAI, M.3091/1852/92.

70 Malet, *The Kirwan case*, pp 93–5.

71 Ibid.

72 Malet, *The Kirwan case*, pp 90–2.

73 NLI, PD2085TX (16).

74 Malet, *The Kirwan case*, pp 90–2.

75 Henry Reeve (ed.), Charles C.F. Greville, *The Greville memoirs: a journal of the reigns of King George IV, King William IV and Queen Elizabeth, vol. 6* (Cambridge, 2011), p. 242.

76 Donal A. Kerr, *'A nation of beggars'?: priests, people and politics in Famine Ireland 1846–1852* (Oxford, 1994), pp 105–6.

77 Michael Barry, *Victorian Dublin revealed: the remarkable legacy of 19th-century Dublin* (Dublin, 2011) p. 82; Martin Maguire, 'The Church of Ireland and the problem of the Protestant working class of Dublin, 1870s–1930s' in Alan Ford, James McGuire and Kenneth Milne (eds), *As by law established, the Church of Ireland since the Reformation* (Dublin, 1995), pp 195–203; Barry, *Victorian Dublin revealed*, p. 82.

78 Barry, *Victorian Dublin revealed*, p. 82.

79 Dickson, *Dublin*, pp 336–9; Barry, *Victorian Dublin revealed*, p. 82.

80 Boswell, *Defence of William Burke Kirwan*, p. 12.

81 Ibid.

82 Jacqueline Hill, 'The language and symbolism of conquest in Ireland, 1790–1850', *Transactions of the Royal Historical Society*, 5th ser. 18 (2008), 165–86.

83 Michael Foley, 'Colonialism and journalism in Ireland', *Journalism Studies*, 5:3 (2004), 373–85; *TN*, 25 Dec. 1852.

84 Helen Hatton, *The largest amount of good: Quaker relief in Ireland, 1654–1921* (London, 1993), p. 146.

85 *TN*, 25 Dec. 1852; Malet, *The Kirwan case*, pp 90–2.

86 *DN*, 14 Jan. 1852.

87 *WM*, 12 Jan. 1853.

88 *DMR*, 26 Oct. 1840; Foley, 'Colonialism and journalism', 376.

89 Maurice Earls, 'The politics of assimilation', *Dublin Review of Books*, March 2007 available at Dublin Review of Books (http://www.drb. Irish Examiner/essays/the-politics-of-assimilation) (accessed 25 Mar. 2016).

90 *CSR*, 19 Jan. 1853; *DEP*, 13 Jan. 1853; Foley, 'Colonialism and journalism', 377.

91 *IE*, 7 Jan. 1853.

92 *CSR*, 13 Jan. 1853.

93 Ibid.

94 A. Daly, 'The Dublin medical press and medical authority in Ireland: 1850–1890' (PhD, NUI, Maynooth, 2008).

95 Tony Farmar, *Patients, potions and physicians: a social history of medicine in Ireland, 1654–2004* (Dublin, 2004), pp 83–4.

96 Ibid.

97 Gordon Wolstenholme, 'The Victorian era' in Eoin O'Brien, Anne Crookshank and Gordon Wolstenholme (eds), *A portrait of Irish medicine: an illustrated history of medicine in Ireland* (Dublin, 1984), pp 115–46.

98 Barry, *Victorian Dublin revealed*, pp 38–9.

99 Wolstenholme, 'The Victorian era', p. 117; Davis Coakley, *Irish masters of medicine* (Dublin, 1992), p. 146.

100 Greta Jones and Elizabeth Malcolm (eds), *Medicine disease and the state, 1650–1940* (Cork 1999); Daly, 'Dublin Medical press'.

101 Eoin O'Brien, *Conscience and conflict: a biography of Sir Dominic Corrigan, 1802–1880* (Dublin, 1983), pp 13–15.

102 Coakley, *Irish masters*, p. 148.

103 Ibid., p. 150.

104 Farmar, *Patients, potions and physicians*, p. 94.

105 Wolstenholme, 'The Victorian era', pp 120–1.

106 Farmar, *Patients, potions and physicians*, pp 80–1.

107 Barry, *Victorian Dublin revealed*, p. 39; Farmar, *Patients, potions and physicians*, pp 80–1; Helen Andrews, 'Marsh, Sir Henry', in *DIB*; Helen Andrews, 'Adams, Robert' in *DIB*.

108 Prof. J.H. Widdess, 'William Wallace (1791–1837)', *British Journal of Venereal Disease*, 41:9 (1965) 9–14.

109 RS Morton, 'Dr. William Wallace (1791–1837) of Dublin', *Medical History*, 10:1 (1966) 38–43.

110 NLI, 2085TX(108).

111 Wolstenholme, 'The Victorian era', p. 127.

112 E. O'Brien, 'Victorian society in Merrion Square', *Heartwise*, 2 (1999), 21–2.

113 Ibid.

114 Armstrong, *Report of the trial of William Burke Kirwan*, pp 61–4; ibid., pp 58–61; Malet, *The Kirwan case*, p. 110; Boswell, *Defence of William Bourke Kirwan*, p. 46.

115 Boswell, *Defence of William Bourke Kirwan*, p. 46.

116 Vaughan, *Murder trials in Ireland*, p. 370.

117 Cyril Wecht, 'The history of legal Medicine', *Journal of the American Academy of Psychiatry and the Law Online*, 33:2 (2005), 245–51.

118 Farmar, *Patients, potions and physicians*, p. 88.

119 Katherine D. Watson, 'Medical and chemical expertise in English trials for criminal poisoning, 1750–1914', *Medical History*, 50:3 (2006), 373–90; Vaughan, *Murder trials in Ireland*, p. 370.

120 Armstrong, *Report of the trial of William Burke Kirwan*, p. 55; *FJ*, 12 Jan. 1853.

121 Petition of J.O. Turnball, St Albans, 8 Jan. 1853, TNA, HO18/349/1852; Petition of John Cameron and Thomas Grimsdale on behalf of the Medical Society of Liverpool, 6 Jan. 1853, TNA, HO18/349/1852.

122 Geoghegan, *An examination of the medical facts*.

123 Malet, *The Kirwan case*, p. 110.

124 M.P. Earles, 'Taylor, Alfred Swaine (1806–1880)', *Oxford dictionary of national biography* (Oxford, 2004); Malet, *The Kirwan case*, pp 110–11; Helen Andrews, 'Neligan, John Moore' in *DIB*.

125 Vaughan, *Murder trials in Ireland*, p. 370.

126 Armstrong, *Report of the trial of William Burke Kirwan*, pp 25–8.

127 *BNL*, 31 Dec. 1852.

128 Watson, 'Medical and chemical expertise in English trials', 376.

129 John Gamble, *Society and manners in early nineteenth-century Ireland* (Dublin, 2011), p. 28.

3. SARAH KIRWAN AND THE ROLE OF MIDDLE-CLASS WOMEN IN SOCIETY

1 Armstrong, *Report of the trial of William Burke Kirwan*, p. 89.

2 Malet, *The Kirwan case*, pp 90–2.

3 Ibid.

4 Ibid., pp 95–6.

5 M.R. Lee, 'The Solanaceae III: henbane, hags and Hawley Harvey Crippen', *Journal of the Royal College of Physicians in Edinburgh*, 36:4 (Dec. 2006), 366–73.

6 A. Anahita Alizadeh, M. Moshiri, J. Alizadeh, and M Balali-Mood, 'Black henbane and its toxicity – a descriptive review', *Avicenna Journal of Phytomedecine*, 4:5 (Sept. 2014), 297–311.

7 *The Pharmacopoeia of the King and Queen's College of Physicians in Ireland* (Dublin, 1850), p. 159; Christopher Hibbert, *Queen Victoria, a personal history* (London, 2009), p. 488; R.V. Pierce, *The people's common sense medical advisor in plain English or medicine simplified* (New York, 1876), p. 344.

8 John K. Crellin and Jane Phillpott, *A reference guide to medicinal plants, herbal medicine past and present* (London, 1990), pp 171–3; ibid., p. 376.

9 Thomas Andrew, *A cyclopedia of domestic medicine and surgery: being an alphabetical account of the various diseases incident to the human frame, with directions for the more simple operations of surgery* (Edinburgh, 1842), pp 346–7; Michael Castleman, *The new healing herbs: the essential guide to more Than 125 of nature's most potent herbal remedies* (3rd ed. New York, 2009), pp 410–11; ibid., pp 173–5.

10 Malet, *The Kirwan case*, pp 90–2; Patricia Vertinskey, *The eternally wounded woman: women, doctors and exercise in the late nineteenth century* (Manchester, 1994), p. 82.

11 Dympna McLoughlin, 'Women and sexuality in nineteenth-century Ireland', *Irish Journal of Psychology*, 15:2 & 3 (1994), 266–75.

12 Malet, *The Kirwan case*, p. 13.

13 M.F. Cusack, *Women's work in modern society* (London, 1874) cited in Maria Luddy (ed.), *Women in Ireland, 1800–1918, a documentary history* (Cork, 1995), p. 15.

14 Katherine Gleadle, *British women in the nineteenth century* (New York, 2001), p. 84.

15 Armstrong, *Report of the trial of William Burke Kirwan*, pp 14–15, p. 67.

16 Malet, *The Kirwan case*, p. 13.

17 Armstrong, *Report of the trial of William Burke Kirwan*, p. 15.

18 Statement of Maria Byrne, NAI, M.3091/1852/91; Malet, *The Kirwan case*, p. 92.

19 NAI, M.3091/1852/91.

20 Armstrong, *Report of the trial of William Burke Kirwan*, p. 61, p. 91.

21 Malet, *The Kirwan case*, pp 93–5.

22 Statement of Mrs Gillas, NAI, M.3091/1852/70.

23 Ibid.

24 Statement of Catherine Kelly, NAI, M.3091/1852/72.

25 NAI, M.3091/1852/70; NAI, M.3091/1852/72.

26 Elizabeth Steiner-Scott, '"To bounce a boot off her now and then", domestic violence in post-Famine Ireland' in Maryann Valiulis and Mary O'Dowd (eds), *Women and Irish history: essays in honour of Margaret MacCurtain* (Dublin, 1997), pp 125–43.

27 24 & 25 Vict., c. 100 [U.K.] (6 August 1861); Mark Finnane, 'A decline in violence in Ireland? Crime, policing and social relations, 1860–1914', *Crime, History & Society*, 1:1 (1997), 51–70.

28 Conley, *Melancholy accidents*, p. 64.

29 Steiner-Scott, '"To bounce a boot off her"', pp 125–43; Conley, *Melancholy accidents*, pp 69–70; Finnane, 'A decline in violence?', 60.

30 Conley, *Melancholy accidents*, pp 69–70.

31 Diane Urquhart, 'Irish divorce and domestic violence', *Women's History Review*, 22:5 (2013), 820–37.

32 Ibid.

33 Keith Thomas, 'The double standard', *Journal of the History of Ideas*, 20:2 (April

1959), 195–216; McLoughlin, 'Women and sexuality', 266.

34 Malet, *The Kirwan case*, p. 31.

35 McLoughlin, 'Women and sexuality', 267; Boswell, *Defence of William Bourke Kirwan*, pp 34–6.

36 Ibid., p. 3.

37 Diane Urquhart, 'Irish divorce and domestic violence', 822.

38 Diane Urquhart, 'Ireland and the divorce and matrimonial causes act of 1857', *Journal of Family History*, 38:3 (2013), 301–20.

39 Ibid.; Mary Lyndon Shanley, '"One must ride behind": married women's rights and the Divorce Act of 1857', *Victorian Studies*, 25:3 (1982), 355–76.

40 Mary Poovey, 'Covered but not bound: Caroline Norton and the 1857 Matrimonial Causes Act', *Feminist Studies*, 14:3 (1988) 467–85; Caroline Norton, *English laws for women in the nineteenth century* (London, 1854).

41 Pam Hirsch, 'Bodichon, Barbara Leigh Smith (1827–1891)' in *Oxford dictionary of national biography*; Barbara Leigh Smith, *A brief summary in plain language of the most important laws concerning women together with a few observations thereon* (London, 1856).

42 Lyndon Shanley, '"One must ride behind"', 360–3.

43 Urquhart 'Ireland, divorce, matrimonial causes', 303; Lyndon Shanley, '"One must ride behind"', 369.

44 Mary Lyndon Shanley, *Feminism, marriage and the law in Victorian England* (Princeton, 1993), pp 104–9.

45 Urquart, 'Irish divorce and domestic violence', 829.

46 Ibid., 830.

47 Boswell, *Defence of William Bourke Kirwan*, pp 34–6.

48 *LCE*, 2 Feb. 1853.

49 Statement of Theresa Kenny, NAI, M.3091/1852/82.

50 McLoughlin, 'Women and sexuality', 271–2.

51 Ibid.

52 Boswell, *Defence of William Bourke Kirwan*, pp 34–36; *CC*, 3 Feb. 1853.

53 McLoughlin, 'Women and sexuality', 273.

54 Diarmuid Ferriter, *Occasions of sin, sex and society in modern Ireland* (London, 2009), p. 22.

55 *NG*, 17 Aug. 1853.
56 Henry Downes Bowyer to the Lords Commissioners of Her Majesty's Treasury, 4 Nov. 1863, NAI, HO18/349/1852.
57 *NG*, 17 Aug. 1853.
58 Ibid.
59 *SNL*, 7 Feb. 1854.
60 *SRCCC*, 29 Nov. 1853.
61 *CJEA*, 17 Apr. 1854; 11 Dec. 1854.
62 McCarthy and Ó Donnabháin, *Too beautiful*, p. 108.
63 Gibson, *Life among convicts*, p. 43; Bodkin, *Great Irish trials*, p. 128.
64 NAI, 1/11/23/1; 'History of Cobh' available at: Cobh: The Queenstown Story, Cobh Heritage Centre (www.cobhheritage.com/cobh/) (accessed 8 Jan. 2016).
65 *FJ*, 8 Feb. 1879.

4. THE LAW, TRANSPORTATION AND IMPRISONMENT

1 Ferdinand Whittingham, *Bermuda, a colony, a fortress, and a prison or eighteen months in the Somers' Islands* (London, 1857), pp iii–iv.
2 David Bentley, *English criminal justice in the nineteenth century* (London, 1998), p. 285.
3 Ibid.
4 *FJ*, 22 Dec. 1852.
5 Mr I. Butt, New trials in criminal cases, 1 June 1853, vol. 27 in *Hansard* 3, i [etc.] *Hansard's parliamentary debates*, 3rd series, 1830–91 (vols i–ccclvi, London, 1831–91).
6 Ibid.
7 *IE*, 15 Jan. 1853.
8 Butt, New trials in criminal cases.
9 Bentley, *English criminal justice*, p. 296.
10 Ibid.; Tom O'Malley, 'Ireland' in Nicola Padfield, Dirk Van Zyl Smit, Frieder Dünke (eds), *Release from prison: European policy and practice* (Cullompton, 2010), p. 228.
11 Clare Anderson, 'Bermuda 1823–1863' available at: Convict Voyages: A Global History of convicts and penal colonies, (http://convictvoyages.org/expert-essays/convicts-in-bermuda) (accessed 4 Jan. 2016).
12 The Convict Establishment at Bermuda, earl of Carnarvon, 26 July 1860 in *Hansard* 3, i, *Hansard's parliamentary debates*, 3rd series, 1830–91 (vols i–ccclvi, London, 1831–91).
13 Anderson, 'Bermuda 1823–1863'.
14 The Convict Establishment at Bermuda, earl of Carnarvon.
15 William Burke Kirwan, Petition to Sir George Grey, Colonial Secretary, 4 Dec. 1861, TNA, HO18/349/1852; William Burke Kirwan, Petition to Sir George Grey, Colonial Secretary, 4 Aug. 1862, TNA, HO18/349/1852.
16 Whittingham, *Bermuda, a colony*, pp 215–18; Gibson, *Life among convicts*, p. 46.
17 Ibid.
18 Whittingham, *Bermuda, a colony*, p. 218.
19 John Mitchell, *Jail journal* (Dublin, 1854).
20 Ibid., p. 74.
21 William Burke Kirwan, Petition to Sir George Grey, 4 Aug. 1862, TNA, HO18/349/1852.
22 M. Heather Tomlinson, 'Penal servitude 1846–1865: a system in evolution' in Victor Bailey (ed.), *Policing and punishment in nineteenth-century Britain* (London, 1981), p. 139.
23 William Burke Kirwan, Petition to Sir George Grey, Colonial Secretary, 29 Apr. 1860, TNA, HO18/349/1852.
24 McCarthy and Ó Donnabháin, *Too beautiful*, p. 228; Motions for Correspondence, earl of Eglington, 13 June 1861, vol. 163 in *Hansard* 3, i, *Hansard Parliamentary Debates*, 3rd series, 1830–91 (vols i–cccivi, London 1831–91).
25 Ibid.
26 William Burke Kirwan, Petition to Sir George Grey, Colonial Secretary, 29 Apr. 1860, TNA, HO18/349/1852.
27 Ibid.
28 Thomas Larcom to Prison Governer, Bermuda Convict Establishment, 1 Nov. 1860, TNA, HO18/349/1852.
29 General Prisons Office, Letter Book, H. Hitchens to Major Larcom, 30 July 1853, NAI, GPO/LB/3; Anderson, 'Bermuda 1823–1863'; Steven Constantine, *Community and identity: the making of modern Gibraltar since 1704* (Oxford, 2009), p. 156.
30 H. Hitchens to Governor of Spike Island, 31 Mar. 1854, NAI, GPO/LB/3.

31 William Burke Kirwan, Petition to Sir George Grey, Colonial Secretary, 4 Dec. 1861, 4 Aug. 1862, 23 Dec. 1862, 15 Apr. 1863, TNA, HO18/349/1852; Isaac Butt to Sir George Grey, 21 Jan. 1862, TNA, HO18/349/1852.

32 Thomas Larcom to Bermuda Convict Establishment, 9 May 1863, TNA, HO18/349/1852.

33 Tomlinson, 'Penal Servitude 1846–1865', p. 132.

34 Sir Stafford Northcote to Lord Grey, 18 Mar. 1864, vol. 173, in *Hansard* 3, i [etc.] *Hansard's parliamentary debates*, 3rd series, 1830–91 (vols i–ccclvi, London, 1831–91).

35 Convict Establishment to the duke of Newcastle, 25 Dec. 1862, TNA, HO18/349/1852.

36 TNA, HO18/349/1852.

37 Sean McConville, *A history of English prison administration* (Oxford, 1981), p. 395.

38 W.B. Kirwan, Millbank Prison to the Home Office, Apr. 1863, TNA, HO18/349/1852.

39 Thomas Larcom to the Home Office, 9 May 1863, TNA, HO18/349/1852.

40 Larcom to Home Office, 9 May 1863, TNA, HO18/349/1852; Notation, Thomas Larcom to the Home Office, 13 May 1863, TNA, HO18/349/1852.

41 Thomas Larcom to Spike Island, 2 May 1854, NAI, GPO/LB/6; *CE*, 11 May 1863; NAI, 1/11/23/1.

42 Cullen, *Dublin 1847*, p. 3; *WFJ*, 24 Dec. 1842.

43 Ibid.

44 Thomas Larcom Papers, Correspondence, 1835–46, on various aspects of the Ordnance Survey, threatening letters to Larcom from 'Capt. Rock', and the murder of Alfred Lynch, supposed to have been committed by Kirwan, NLI, MS 7519.

45 Ibid.

46 *CE*, 12 Jan. 1853.

5. VICTORIAN MORAL CODES AND NEWSPAPER REPORTING

1   *CE*, 29 Dec. 1852.

2   Armstrong, *Report of the trial of William Burke Kirwan*, p. 4.

3   Ibid., p. 56.

4   'The murderer's Christmas', *IE*, 29 Dec. 1852; *TN*, 11 Dec. 1852.

5   Judith Rowbottom and Kim Stevenson, *Criminal conversations: Victorian crimes, social panic and moral outrage* (Ohio, 2005), p. xxiv.

6   *TN*, 15 Jan. 1853; *FJ*, 13 Jan. 1853; *DEM*, 13 Jan. 1853.

7   *DEM*, 3 Jan. 1853; *LES*, 13 Dec. 1852; *AC*, 16 Dec. 1852.

8   *BNL*, 12 Jan. 1853.

9   *FJ*, 17 Sept. 1853; *DEM*, 10 Jan. 1853.

10 *BNL*, 12 Jan. 1853

11 Ibid.

12 *CE*, 8 Jan. 1853.

13 *FJ*, 27 Sept. 1843.

14 Ibid., 12 Jan. 1853.

15 John Knight Boswell, *Exposure of an attempt to impute the murder of Messrs. Crowe and Bowyer to W.B. Kirwan* (Dublin, 1853), pp 3–5.

16 Ibid.

17 *CE*, 13 July 1853.

18 NAI, M.3091/1852/91; Malet, *The Kirwan case*, pp 90–2; Boswell, *Exposure of an attempt*, p. 5

19 Ibid., p. 3; *LCE*, 19 Jan. 1853.

20 Laurel Brake and Marysa Demoor (eds), *Dictionary of nineteenth-century journalism in Great Britain and Ireland* (London, 2009), pp 152–3.

21 Ibid.

22 For examples see *FJ*, 24 Jan. 1850; *IE*, 9 Sept. 1850; *BNL*, 18 June 1850, 10 Oct. 1851 & 31 Oct. 1851; *IE*, 27 May 1850; 24 Sept. 1852.

23 *BNL*, 16 Sept. 1853.

24 *CE*, 15 Dec. 1852; *DWN*, 11 Dec. 1852.

25 Carolyn Conley, *Certain other countries: homicide, gender and national identity in late nineteenth-century England, Ireland, Scotland and Wales* (Ohio, 2007), p. 67.

26 *UM*, 15 Dec. 1852.

27 Vaughan, *Murder trials in Ireland*, pp 387–90.

28 Conley, *Certain other countries*, pp 91–2.

29 Conley, *Melancholy accidents*, pp 63–7.

30 *DEPC*, 17 Mar. 1853; *EF*, 8 Aug. 1853; *TC*, 18 Mar. 1850; *DWN*, 12 Mar. 1853.

31 *DEM*, 29 Mar. 1850.

32 *TC*, 29 Mar. 1850.

33 *DEP*, 16 Mar. 1850; *DMA*, 21 Mar. 1851.

34 *FJ*, 15 May 1853.